W9-AYR-401

DAYS OF HUNGER, DAYS OF CHAOS

The Coming Great Food Shortages in America

TEXE MARRS

RCP RiverCrest Publishing
1708 Patterson Road • Austin, Texas 78733

ACKNOWLEDGEMENTS

So many wonderful people deserve credit for their gracious contributions to this book. My precious wife, Wanda, is always a treasure. Her smile and encouragement, ideas and advice, and administrative talents are worth more than tons of silver and gold. Without her this book would have never been published. My superb, dedicated staff must be mentioned—Michelle Delgado for her management skills, help in design on the book's cover and format, and cheery, positive Christian spirit; Anita Gonzales for incomparable typing and editing; and James Lundeen for cover design, art graphics and book formatting. I am grateful to Joe Saldaña and his son, Joseph, for keeping our shipping room humming, and to Gerry Schappert and Shirley Gantt, whose sparkling personalities and computer skills are an asset. My appreciation also to Dollie Hallmark for her administrative assistance and to Sandra Myers of Ambassador House for the exceptional typesetting. Finally, to the many friends of the ministry who stand with me and who pray for us: Thank you and God bless you!

Days of Hunger, Days of Chaos: The Coming Great Food Shortages in America

Copyright © 1999 by Texe Marrs. Published by RiverCrest Publishing, 1708 Patterson Road, Austin, Texas 78733.

All rights reserved. No part of this publication may be reproduced, stored in a retrieval system or transmitted in any form by any means, electronic, mechanical, photocopy, recording, or otherwise, without the prior permission of the publisher, except as provided by USA copyright law.

Scripture quotations are from the King James Version of The Holy Bible.

Cover design: Texe Marrs and James Lundeen
Art on front cover is from the painting by Albert Pinkham Ryder, *Death on a Pale Horse*, the Cleveland Museum of Art, Cleveland, Ohio.

Printed in the United States of America

Library of Congress Catalog Card Number 98-68372

Categories: 1. Current Events and Issues 2. Prophecy
             3. Economics and Money   4. Religion and Bible

ISBN 0-9667421-0-9

DAYS OF HUNGER, DAYS OF CHAOS

*"There shall be famines, and pestilences...
For then shall be great tribulation, such as
was not since the beginning of the world to
this time, no, nor ever shall be...Behold, I
have told you before."*

—*Jesus Our Lord*
Matthew 24:7,21,25

OTHER BOOKS BY TEXE MARRS

Project L.U.C.I.D.: The Beast 666 Universal Human Control System

Circle of Intrigue: The Hidden Inner Circle of the Global Illuminati Conspiracy

Big Sister is Watching You: Hillary Clinton and the White House Feminists Who Now Control America—And Tell the President What to Do

Dark Majesty: The Secret Brotherhood and the Magic of A Thousand Points of Light

Millennium: Peace, Promises, and the Day They Take Our Money Away

America Shattered

New Age Cults and Religions

Mystery Mark of the New Age

Dark Secrets of the New Age

FOR TEXE MARRS' FREE NEWSLETTER

For a free subscription to *Power of Prophecy*, Texe Marrs' international newsletter, please phone toll free (800) 234-9673, or write to:

RiverCrest Publishing
1708 Patterson Road
Austin, Texas 78733

Please e-mail your request to: *prophecy@texemarrs.com*, or visit us at our internet website: *http://www.texemarrs.com*

TABLE OF

Contents

INTRODUCTION

"Behold A Pale Horse"

Often, I have been asked, "What, in your opinion, is the single most frightening and most terrible of all the images found in the prophetic scriptures of the Holy Bible?"

Without hesitation, my response is always the same. To me, *Revelation 6* is by far the most gripping and evocative. From the moment I first heard this passage read aloud in church until today, a half century later, I continue to be both captivated *and* horrified by the dramatic description God has given us of end-times events in the sixth chapter of the book of *Revelation*.

Here is recorded the ultimate in evil and monstrous deeds. Here we see the ominous, dreaded Four Horsemen of the Apocalypse, galloping toward us at full speed, bringing in their wake judgement in the form of savage wars, bloodshed, carnage, famine, hunger and disease.

In breathtaking succession, we envision the image of the rider of the white horse, the red, the black, and, finally, the pale horse. The rider of the pale horse is surely the most terrifying of the four. His very *name* is Death, spelled with a capital letter "D"!—

> And I looked, and behold a pale horse: and his name that sat on him was Death, and Hell followed with him. And power was given unto them over the fourth part of the earth, to kill with sword, and with hunger, and with death..." *(Revelation 6:8)*

Who is this mysterious rider of the pale horse who has the ferocious name, Death? Is Death the name of one person or many? Is Death the Bible's symbolic name for *they*, or *them*, the elite who comprise the aristocratic inner circle of the global conspiracy. Is this why they are so determined to birth an antichrist New World Order in the last days? Certainly, whoever it is that bears the perditious name, Death, we know that all the sinister, demon forces of Hell follow after him. These devils from Hell are imbued with the necessary power, authority, and means to destroy a fourth part of mankind. Their swath of evil through the ranks of the Earth's populace is achieved through sword (war) and with hunger and starvation.

The toll of death prophesied to occur translates into a mind-boggling *one and a half billion unfortunate men, women, and children* who are soon to meet their maker. These victims, as well as you and I, have a rendezvous and appointment with destiny. None of us can avoid this time of destiny. From the beginning of time, God preordained all things and wrote in His book a detailed plan and road map for your life and mine.

God Has Determined

Thus, I begin this book with a penetrating, straight-to-the-point assertion and declaration: God has determined a furious and grim period of intense, overwhelming hunger and death to be visited upon mankind. This will be a breathtaking panorama of destruction and suffering like nothing you and I have ever witnessed or, possibly, can even imagine. Men and women will become so desperate for food they will kill their fellow man and eat his flesh. Some will even cut off their own limbs and eat them.

This gruesome time of hunger and bloodcurdling physical devastation will be preceded by graphic developments of a monumental scale in the financial world. The world economy will collapse, leaving the stock markets in tatters, banks in total ruin, American currency worthless, and hundreds of millions of people in dire straits—demoralized, shocked, hungry, sick, and homeless.

The rapid decline of the dollar and devaluation of foreign currencies will cause prices of food and other consumer goods to plummet and fall. Bread, milk, meat, cereals, and other staples will cost only pennies. Still, little will be found available anywhere, at any price. All foodstuffs will be stored at central distribution points and rationed. Doors of local grocery stores and supermarkets will be padlocked, and shelves will be empty.

Meanwhile, crops will lie rotting in the fields. In a strange and ghastly contradiction, farmers who attempt to harvest their fields will be harshly punished by the authorities.

Panic will seize the hearts of peoples everywhere. Money gone, no food to eat, the world will be brought to its knees. After a brief denial of economic collapse will come the all-consuming specter of famine, disease, and homelessness. The grim future will fill men and women with fear and dread. Soon, anger and frustration will break out. Formerly law-abiding citizens will turn on one another, even brother against brother, in a violent rampage and scramble for food and survival.

Federal Authorities Swing Into Action

A chain of rapid-fire events will take place. The President, with the full approval of Congress and heeding the cries of the public who fear for their safety, will declare *martial law*. The Federal Emergency Management Agency (FEMA) will activate detention camps for rioters, looters, food hoarders, and pre-identified, potential "government resisters."

The United Nations Security Council, in emergency session, will empower its World Food Organization to take over the planet's food production and distribution. Every nation, province, state, city, town, and village will have a Food Council. This will be a small group of collective powerbrokers designated by the authorities as legally and morally responsible for the rationing, storage and distribution of food.

Food Councils will decree that only those citizens with the mark, or name, or the number of the name of the global leader, may buy or sell food and other life necessities. This rule will be promulgated in the name of uniformity and fairness, to cause peoples everywhere to share food, and to prevent hoarding of limited resources.

Dissenters to the new laws and regulations, especially *food criminals*, will be brutally dealt with. Summary courts, with judges appointed by an International Criminal Court, will possess the delegated authority to try violators and carry out immediate executions. Instant death by beheading will be universal punishment for infractions. After all, why feed and house these troublemakers, these useless eaters, and thus waste precious commodities in exceedingly short supply?

Thus will be fulfilled the ominous prophecy of *Revelation 13:15* that, in the end times, the authorities shall have the awesome power to "cause that as many as would not worship the image of the beast should be killed."

Black-clothed and ski-masked police SWAT teams will conduct roundup after roundup of suspected terrorists and "antigovernment types." The National Guard and the military will assist in house to house firearms confiscation and checks of home kitchen pantries and storage areas, to root out those who are guilty of hoarding food. Those who are caught— who have more than their share of allotted food—will be taken away. Some of the "criminals" will have their faces shown on television, and the public will be encouraged to express its utter contempt and hatred for these "vile, selfish specimens of human trash."

It will further be viewed by the majority as doing God service when this human trash is done away with. This will fulfill Jesus prophecy that, "whosoever killeth you will think that he doeth God service." (*John 16:2*)

Saviors of Mercy

This untamed lust for the blood of sacrificial victims as scapegoats, purposely inspired in the hearts of the wicked, will cause the people of all nations to revere and honor as "saviours of mercy" the god-men who rule over them. In doing, so they will also be paying homage to Satan, the dragon, who infuses these men and their global system of human control with such terrible power and authority:

> And they worshipped the dragon which gave power unto the beast: and they worshipped the beast, saying, Who is like unto the beast? who is able to make war with him?... and power was given him over all kindreds, and tongues, and nations. (*Revelation 13:4,7*)

Premonitions of Evil to Come

Are the events predicted above too preposterous to contemplate? Do you doubt for a moment that everything mentioned here will transpire? Please, I beg you to understand: Already, in this century alone, the Lord has given you and I premonitions of the horrendous evil to come. The seeds have been sown.

We have only to look to recent history to glimpse what horrors lie just ahead. Consider the food famine in the Ukraine. If you had lived in the Ukraine in the 1930s, you very likely would have become a blood-drenched victim of one of the biggest acts of genocide in the annals of human history. The Communists drove Ukraine farmers and their families into collectives, robbing them of their lands and their homes. Stalin then purged and massacred between five and twenty million people in the Ukraine alone.

In Germany in the 40s, as a Bible-believing Christian or Jew you would likely have become an inmate at one of the many Nazi concentration camps that have since been legitimately dubbed by historians as "killing factories." Your body may well have been consumed to ashes in a crematoria furnace.

If, in the 1970s in Cambodia when the Communist *Khmer Rouge* seized control, you had been a high school graduate, a former government employee, or a sick and disabled person, you would certainly have ended up bludgeoned to death by a baseball bat, your body discarded in a pyramidal heap of bones. Before your untimely death, you could have been one of the tens of thousands unmercifully tortured in a dungeon-like "reeducation center."

In the 1990s, being of the Tutsi tribe in the African nation of Rwanda was a ticket to dismemberment by a machete. In Eastern Europe, in Bosnia and former Yugoslavia, if you had the misfortune to be a Croat or a Moslem and you were captured by the Serb opposition, a bullet-hole in the head and a bulldozed pit could have been your fate.

Neither has the U.S.A. been an oasis of peace. If you were unfortunate enough in April of 1993 to have been an innocent and harmless child or a baby in the besieged Branch Davidian building in Waco, Texas, you would have been frightened, starved and otherwise tormented for days on end. Then, you and your parents would have been gassed, and either shot, asphyxiated, or burned to death by ruthless federal agents of the FBI and BATF.

Government Executioners and Torturers

In each of these gross instances of inhumane atrocities, the perpetrators of terror and genocide were not dissident groups of rebels or radical, antigovernment terrorists. The executioners and torturers were *government* and *government agents*. As the world moves fast-forward into the dawning of a new millennium, the principal proponents of state-sponsored genocide and murder are government leaders who were actually chosen for their political posts by the citizenry. Most hold high office as a result of democratic elections, just as Hitler was democratically elected as Germany's Chancellor by a majority vote of the populace.

The state persecutors of humanity are prideful and arrogant. They have the intelligence service, the secret police, and the corrupt justice system in their employ. They vainly quest for even more money and ever greater totalitarian powers, and they kill and hurt those who resist or complain about government injustice.

On this earth, for a time, evil men such as this shall have their reward. Yet, being motivated by devils, these men will in turn, ultimately be consumed and destroyed. As we read in *Psalms 10:2*, "The wicked in his pride doth persecute the poor; let them be taken in the devices that they have imagined." And we read, "He that diggeth a pit shall fall into it." (*Ecclesiastes 10:8*)

Contrived, Pre-planned Crises

Moreover, it should be realized that the coming great time of hunger and chaos will not happen as a result of accidental, neutral circumstances. This will be a planned series of events, a contrived succession of crises, an engineered emergency designed to create conditions for the implementation of revolutionary government and the initiation of a radiant New Civilization.

It will not be the first time that the Illuminist elite have engineered and taken advantage of political, social and economic chaos. In the 1940s, Congressmen Louis McFadden, then Chairman of the House Committee on Banking and Currency, emphatically stated:

> It (the Depression) was not accidental. It was a carefully contrived occurrence. The international bankers sought to

bring about a condition of despair so that they might emerge the rulers of us all.[1]

For his impudence in exposing the facts about the Great Depression, McFadden was severely attacked by the monied interests. The Congressman met an untimely and most mysterious demise. Some maintain he was secretly murdered.

Heroes Alive Today

Today, I believe there are still heroes alive—men and women who, like McFadden, refuse to bow before the altar of expediency. These are men and women who refuse to worship the beast or kowtow to the corrupt world system. Though such heroes may be few, their courageous exploits and untold victories shall for all eternity be cited as prime examples of goodness, idealism, and self-sacrifice. The amazing truth is that these heroic men and women are glorious inheritors of the Kingdom of God. Such people do not seek fame or acclaim. They care not for contemporary advantage, but, rather, they strive to please their Lord and Saviour in Heaven.

These are they which fear God, but fear neither man nor devil. And because of their faith and hope, they shall be amply and magnificently rewarded by He who holds the key to life and death. His eye is upon them and, in perilous time of famine and death, they shall live:

> Behold, the eye of the Lord is upon them that fear him, upon them that hope in his mercy; To deliver their soul from death, to keep them alive in famine. (*Psalms 33:18-19*)

> They will not be ashamed in the time of evil; and in the days of famine they shall be satisfied. (*Psalms 37:19*)

> He is their strength in time of trouble. And the Lord shall help them, and deliver them; he shall deliver them from

the wicked, and save them, because they trust in him.
(Psalms 37:39-40)

Are you prepared for the long prophesied and now emergent
Days of Hunger, Days of Chaos? If you desire refuge, you
must rely on the Lord of glory. You must believe in Him and
come to the cross. In the savage days just ahead, he who
attempts to save his life will lose it, but he who trusts in Him
and turns his life over to God will save it. Whoever does not
have Jesus will lose everything. But he who has Jesus will
possess the riches of ages past and of all ages to come.

> *"Rich men have, indeed, always despised the poor, and now, at last, they have discovered the ultimate means to suppress and dominate the less fortunate. The elite conspirators have developed a fantastically multifaceted plan to take over and manage the food supply for planet Earth. The final struggle, the final war, will be fought not with aircraft, bombs, and bullets, but with food. 'He who has the food wins'—that is the new motto of the Illuminati."*

1

The Coming Great Hunger

There is coming a brutish time of severe food shortages in America. No matter what your circumstances, you will be affected. There will be little or no food at any price. What limited food supplies do remain will be strictly controlled by government authorities. Food will be rationed by law, and you and I will be allowed to purchase only our meager portion. Moreover, your plea to buy food will be refused by the authorities unless your name and number are found in the *World Food Authority's* central computer database.

I repeat: Food shortages are soon to become painfully evident in America. The specter of famine will loom large in our lives. The bible prophesies it. But how, we ask ourselves, will this transpire? What forces will be set in motion to accomplish it? Will the coming days of hunger and starvation be the result of monumental acts of God—like killer hurricanes, floods, and droughts; or viruses and natural pestilences attacking our crops? Could such a drama of unheralded human misery unfold as a by product of general nuclear war?...or of an unexpected, deadly comet or meteor smashing into Earth from outer space?

Planned Acts of Selfish and Greedy Men

Certainly, God can cause these shattering types of Earth-changing events to occur. But, based upon careful analysis and years of meticulous research, I now believe that the period of mass hunger on the way will come about because of the *planned* acts of selfish and greedy men. Yes, evil, devilish men. Seeking power and domination over their fellowmen, these evil schemers have decided to use food as a weapon.

It is their plan to gain total world power through their control of the production, storage, distribution, and sale of food. Food, they are convinced, translates into empire.

We will see in later chapters of this book that, amazing as it may seem to the average American—brainwashed and brain-dead as he or she is due to television and media propaganda—secret units of our own federal government have already set up a structure of control over the food production and supply system. Spy satellites in the sky overhead are now monitoring what farmers are planting. Weather modification weapons are being employed to cause intermittent floods and droughts. The World Trade Organization is establishing quotas and new guidelines for food quality for farmers.

The conspiratorial elite have bought up vast land holdings and have locked up agricultural resources in America. Steadily, they are driving the small, family farmers out of business.

Their multinational, corporate conglomerates own beef, pork, and chicken processing plants and they hold important, exclusive patents on seeds. They own the chemical plants that manufacture commercial fertilizer. They run the money center banks that can make or break the small farmer through the debt process, and they have their men in the White House and in the Congress as chairmen of the appropriate congressional committees overseeing banking, trade, commerce, and agriculture.

Everything is now in place for the kickoff of the cardinal event—an unparalleled crisis and emergency situation that will result in global food scarcity. This will set off a terrible, all-consuming panic as shocked Americans discover that their supermarkets have no groceries on the shelves. Such a thing has never happened in our lifetime. The Great Depression of the 30s, when hunger was so prevalent, is but a faded memory. Since infancy, the typical American alive today has been spoiled and pampered, and has never seen hard times. When the coming Great Hunger is upon us, all hell is going to break loose.

You can count on a frantic public to demand that political leaders immediately do something, *anything*, to resolve the crisis, to insure survival and get food to the people. Indeed, the alarmed citizenry will not hesitate to give up their rights, liberties, and freedoms in exchange for the security of just having bread on the table. Anyone—or any group—that gets in the way of the restoration of economic prosperity and the provision of food to the masses will be hated and despised.

At exactly such times as this, dictators and totalitarian systems rise to the fore and capture the people's rabid support with their ready-made, decisive solutions. This will be the time for the prophesied Fourth Kingdom and its antichrist ruler to emerge:

> Thus he said, The fourth beast shall be the fourth kingdom upon earth, which shall be diverse from all kingdoms, and shall devour the whole earth, and shall tread it down, and break it in pieces.

The 1930s Great Depression brought untold human suffering and misery to tens of millions of Americans. Hunger spread far and wide as once fertile, but now parched and dry, fields crumbled to dust. Eventually, crops dried up and shriveled. Soup lines were set up in major cities to feed the unemployed. The super-rich, however,—the Rockefellers, Rothschilds, and others—successfully consolidated their holdings, became immensely wealthier, and were able to further their ultimate aim of total economic domination via government socialism.

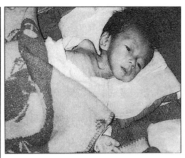

Over the past few decades the United States has enjoyed unparalleled economic prosperity. But the Bible prophesies global famine and pestilence in the end-times. America will not be exempt from great food shortages. In many nations and regions, famine, disease, and death already now stalk whole populations. Above left, a young African woman in Biafra prepares a dead rat for cooking and eating. (In the picture, the woman's face is covered up, to prevent embarrassment.) In African countries—such as Ethiopia, Chad, Liberia, Eritrea, Somalia, Rwanda, and Biafra—many people have survived on snakes, rats, mice, insects, and bitter roots.

    In the late 1990s, in North Korea on the continent of Asia, millions perished during the grim ravages of famine. At top right, a severely malnourished child is cared for at a relief clinic in North Korea.

    At lower right, in Manila, the Phillipines, people pick over the rubbish in a garbage dump, searching for edible food and for anything of value.

And the ten horns out of this kingdom are ten kings that
shall arise: and another shall rise after them; and he shall
be diverse from the first, and he shall subdue three kings.

And he shall speak great words against the most High,
and shall wear out the saints of the most High, and think
to change times and laws: and they shall be given into his
hand until a time and times and the dividing of times.
(Daniel 7:23-25)

The Elite Take Charge

In my book *Circle of Intrigue: The Hidden Inner Circle of
the Illuminati Conspiracy*, I unmask the designs of the
conspiratorial elite and discuss the ten powerful men ("ten
kings") who are to rule the Fourth Kingdom, the end-times
One World Government prophesied in the biblical books of
Daniel and *Revelation*. To fully comprehend the reasons for
the coming, great scarcity of food, we must carefully examine
the clever maneuvers and manipulations of this elitist group,
a group of men best identified under the code name of the
Illuminati.

The Illuminati is made up of a few men of awesome
mercantile power whose riches and political influence place
them at the very apex, or epicenter, of global authority. Due
to their great riches and the possession of their very souls by
demonic powers, these men have long lusted after power as
an end in itself. Thus, they have continually sought to discover
an ironclad means of controlling and enslaving other men.

The emergence of this conspiratorial elite has not gone
unnoticed, though the vast majority of people are too "politically
correct" and purposely misinformed to know of the
Illuminati's's existence. In *The New Unhappy Lords*, his
keenly interesting guidebook to their existence and operations,
Englishman A.K. Chesterton announces that he has discovered:

...the existence of a conspiracy for the destruction of the

Western world as the prelude for shepherding mankind into a sheep's pen as a prelude to One World tyranny.[1]

Also from Europe come these insightful comments from Frenchman Jean-Marie Le Pen, head of France's National Front Party. Mr. Le Pen has given the establishment politicians who favor the New World Order fits because of his opposition leadership. An astute observer of the globalist's internationalist agenda, Le Pen remarks:

> It is evident that the danger of European Community domination over the world has been replaced by a globalist and mercantile domination. This ideology aims at world government by a small financial oligarchy, backed by the United Nations and the various international enforcement agencies. The proponents of this new world domination consider the nations of the world as their principal enemies. It is their aim to weaken them and then destroy the nations. Once this is accomplished, then will come the reign of "Big Brother," described in (George) Orwell's *1984*...[2]

Mr. Le Pen sounds a warning and a recommendation we should all heed:

> Let us not be mistaken about this: We are witnessing a veritable conspiracy to create global power that would deprive the people of their national independence.[3]

The perceptive American novelist, Taylor Caldwell, once wrote of the schemes of the globalist oligarchy, the men of the Illuminati. Their enemy, she noted, is the middle class, the "little people." The elite are determined that the middle class must be shoved back into the corner.[4]

By their deliberate staging of a massive and dramatic period of world hunger, the Illuminati believe the middle class can be reduced to despair and misery. The sniveling "little people" will then be forced to go to the elite on bended knees begging for the precious few crumbs of bread available.

The late Taylor Caldwell held the middle class, the "little people," in the highest esteem. It is they, she observed, who "made the dream of liberty a possibility, set limits on the government, fought for its constitutions, removed much of governmental privilege and tyranny, and demanded that rulers obey the just laws as closely as the people."[5]

Truly Inferior Dogs to be Suppressed

Taylor Caldwell made the point that the elite are angered and outraged that the ordinary masses have risen up. Arrogantly, they are determined to suppress and to make war against the lower caste. The elite, she says, gathered themselves together and grumbled, "Are we not by birth and money entitled to rule a nation of docile slaves? Do the people not understand that they are truly inferior dogs who need a strong hand to rule over them?"[6]

The elitists, said Caldwell, hate the people with a purple passion, and have resolved to subvert and abolish their restrictive Bill of Rights and put the middle class once again under subjection:

> Little wonder that the elite hated the middle class which challenged them in the name of God-given liberty. And little wonder that this hatred grew deeper as the middle class became stronger and imposed restrictions through which all the people, including the most humble, had the right to rule their own lives and keep the greater part of what they earned for themselves.

> Clearly, if the elite were to rule again, the middle class had to be destroyed so despotism and the system of tribute could be returned, and grandeur and honor and immense riches of the elite—assuring their monopoly rule of all the world.[7]

James, the brother of Jesus, foresaw the blasphemy of the elite and the hatred of these super-rich conspirators toward the ordinary, working man and woman:

> Hearken, my beloved brethren, Hath not God chosen the poor of this world, rich in faith, and heirs of the kingdom which he hath promised to them that love him? But ye have despised the poor. Do not rich men oppress you, and draw you before the judgement seats? Do not they blaspheme that worthy name by which ye are called? (*James 2:5-7*)

"He Who Has the Food Wins"

Rich men have, indeed, always despised the poor, and now, at last, they have discovered the ultimate means to suppress and dominate the less fortunate. The elite conspirators have developed a fantastically multifaceted plan to take over and manage the food supply for planet Earth. The final struggle, the final war, will be fought not with aircraft, bombs, and bullets, but with food. "He who has the food wins"—that is the new motto of the Illuminati.

Their modern-day quest begins with their control of money. They are already the bankers; they hold the purse strings of the world's large, money center banks. They dictate to the Federal Reserve Board, the Bank for International Settlements, the World Bank, the European Monetary Institute, the World Trade Organization, and other jointly managed money, banking, and trade institutions. Through their control of the White House and Congress, the elite also are able to tap into the federal treasury whenever the need arises.

With their money, the Illuminati have acquired immense reserves of agricultural lands. They now own and operate gigantic farming collectives, grain elevators, meat packing and processing plants, and other means of food production. They also own or control the distribution chain—comprised of railroads, barges, truck-lines and ships—by which food commodities are brought to the market.

Their latest acquisition is even more grandiose. It involves the use of the elite's multinational corporations, working in collusion with government researchers, to merge the fields of genetic engineering and seed production. The elite conspirators are on the very threshold of controlling the rights to the use by farmers of the most basic unit of the food supply—the unheralded, but mighty, *seed.*

Without seeds, farmers cannot plant and there can be no crops—and no food for the six billion people on Earth. Thus, the motto, "He who has the food wins," is complemented by the truism that, *"Whoever controls the seeds shall ultimately control the people."*

Ordo Ab Chao

Understanding that food, or the lack thereof, translates into power, the elite have concocted a brilliant stratagem. They will purposely cause chaotic food shortages to occur, and then, they will take advantage of the ensuing chaos to achieve their overriding twin objectives: *total global domination* and *total human control.*

The elite have long realized the latent advantages of *chaos* in achievement of their conspiratorial aims. The operational slogan for the 33rd degree of Freemasonry is, in fact, *Ordo Ab Chao*—Latin for "Order Out of Chaos." Through revolution and chaos, the conspirators succeeded in overturning the Russian Czar in 1917 and installing the Bolshevik Communist regime—thanks to the hidden assistance of Jewish Trotskyite agents from the Bronx, New York. Through revolution and chaos, Mao Tse Tung rose to power in China—thanks to hidden, behind-the-scenes support for Mao's Communist insurgency by President Harry S. Truman and his chief military advisor, General George C. Marshall.

As a World Goodwill publication explains it, the elite are convinced that the New International Economic Order can only come about by the *destruction* of the old order.

Through chaos will emerge a "new creation:"

> In the destruction of the old world order and in the chaos of these modern times, the work of the new creation is going forward; the task of reconstruction, leading to a complete organization of human living, and to a fresh, real orientation of human thinking, is taking place.[8]

The elite and their agents have spawned crisis after crisis in their ongoing campaign to achieve progress through chaos. Ervin Lazlo, Director of the United Nations Institute for Training and Research, has said that all the many crises now confronting mankind—environmental, illegal drugs, terrorism, overpopulation, economic, and political—could profitably bring about "a moment of critical instability" and thus a transformation to a New World Order.[9]

Preparations for this transformational "moment of critical instability" have long been underway, and have especially involved the law enforcement, intelligence services, and military branches of the United States. Recently, a letter to the editor from a former U.S. Army Green Beret was printed in the conservative newsletter, *Straight Talk*. Note particularly the soldier's revealing—and alarming—comments about the CIA training course for soldiers titled, "Methods of Control:"

> In the late 70s, I enlisted in the Army. Eventually, I passed through the 82nd Airborne Division at Fort Bragg, North Carolina. There, I volunteered for Special Forces, was accepted for training, passed and was assigned to an A-team in one of those groups. At the time, President Reagan had replaced President Carter, and activity was increasing. Nicaragua, Sudan, Afghanistan. Delta Force was getting firmly established. The CIA was pulling skilled Green Beret, Special Forces NCO's and officers and giving them special assignments.
>
> During this time, I participated in things which patriots might believe are recent corruptions of the Constitution.

For instance, plain clothes surveillance of civilian citizens. These citizens were not known to have committed any crime and were never aware that they, their friends, or family were being watched. Pictures and notes of travel routes, work places, and homes were recorded.

Sometimes this information would be turned over to a hit team. These guys would work out the best method, time and place to take someone out. Either take him out or snatch them. We were told it was only practice—practice right up to the event. But it was also conditioning us.

Another type of training, given at Smith Lake, Fort Bragg, was intensive weapons training on targets dressed as civilians. This included women and priests. I believe it was further conditioning of us, to remove psychological inhibitions. This was a distant root of Waco.

Lastly, and most chilling, was a class that I attended given by the CIA. We were not allowed to take notes. It didn't register at the time, but does now. The title of the course was *Methods of Control,* known as M.O.C. It was about how to control a population through economic stress, production shortages of material goods, consumption of people's free time, or induced poverty. The key was to keep people barefoot, broke, anxious, exhausted and downtrodden. Sound familiar?

I write this to inform you. Your publication is the best chance to save ourselves and restore our lost liberties. The evil depend upon ignorance. Through correspondence and shared knowledge we can lift the rock these serpents hide under. We're a good people, but this has been a long time coming and we must resist as best we can. Thank you,
—A Patriot (name withheld.)[10]

According to this soldier's testimony, the U.S. Army's Special Forces, also called "Green Berets," were taught by the CIA to "control the population through economic stress... production shortages...material poverty." This certainly fits in with the engineered creation of a devastating food crisis, with the intent to "keep people...broke, anxious, exhausted and downtrodden."

One Vast Ecumenical Holding Company

What is planned for all of us is that we shall be owned body and soul by the Illuminati's "company store"—designed to be a vast, ecumenical holding company which replaces all nations and ideologies, including the United States and its Constitution.

Remarkably, the classic movie, *Network*, starring Peter Fitch and Faye Dunaway, concerned this very theme. The plot focuses on how television and the media assist the super-rich and their commercial Babylon interests by programming and conditioning the docile masses to accept the agenda laid out before them by their controllers. In the most brilliant monologue of the entire movie, a multinational corporate chairman who heads the TV network, Mr. Jensen, lashes out at an idealistic newsman who made the mistake of thinking that the old concepts of Americanism, patriotism, equality, and justice are still valid.

"No", shouted Mr. Jensen to the newsman. "This is a new world, and you will adjust your thinking and behavior and teach the people the new way through the medium of television."

Then the corporate chairman explained to his veteran news anchor exactly how the world works and what will henceforth be expected of him in fulfilling his chosen role of propaganda spokesman:

> You are an old man who thinks in terms of nations and peoples. There are no Russians. There are no nations. There are no peoples....There is only one holistic system of systems, one vast, interwoven, interacting, multivariate, multinational dominion of dollars....That is the atomic,

subatomic and galactic structure of things today...

You get up on your little 21-inch screen and howl about American and democracy....There is no America, there is no democracy. There is only IBM and ITT and AT&T and DuPont and Dow and Union Carbide and Exxon. Those are the nations of the world today. What do you think the Russians talk about in their counsels of state? Karl Marx? They get out their linear programming charts, statistical decision theories, mini-max solutions, and compute the price/cost probabilities of their transactions and investments just like we do.

We no longer live in a world of nations and ideologies... The world is a collage of corporations, inexorably determined by the immutable bylaws of business. The world is a business...and it has been so since man crawled out of the slime...

Our children will live to see that perfect world...one vast ecumenical holding company for whom all men will work to serve a common profit, in which all men will hold a share of stock, all necessities provided, all anxieties tranquilized, all boredom amused. And I have chosen you...to preach this evangel.

In the coming days, when famine and pestilence abound and great numbers of desperate men, women and children are dying of hunger and starvation, our leaders—the politicians who represent the vast global ecumenical holding company— will be there, ready with a tailor-made economic solution. They will promise to restore order out of prevailing chaos. Their solution will be to give the agents of control minutely detailed management authority for all food distribution. The powerful new *World Food Authority* and its many national and local subsidiaries will be born. A computerized and well-armed global and federal police force will keep law and order, quell dissidents, and restore public safety and security.

And our lives will never again be the same.

Unbeknownst to the majority of everyday Americans, the world conspiracy is real. Its long-cherished goal is the flesh and soul domination of ordinary men and women whom the elite consider to be their racial and social inferiors. For centuries, the Illuminati and their predecessors have conspired and collectively toiled in secret to enslave humanity. Their aim has always been to usher in a political, economic, and religious system which would permanently guarantee their divine right to rule over the common citizen. They seek nothing less than to control and possess the material world and to cause men's gazes to veer from the face of the one, true, living God.

Until now, these men have been thwarted in fulfilling their debauched conspiratorial objectives. Incredibly, they now realize that, through the manipulation, control, and denial of food to the teeming masses, they can finally attain that total degree of power for which they have labored so diligently and so long.

Fascinating Questions Answered in this Book

In the succeeding pages, we will examine the plan of the conspiratorial elite to drive the world into a Fascist system of human economic and social control by artificially creating food shortages and generating mass hunger and famine. Here are just some of the fascinating questions this book will answer in its investigation into the coming, great food crisis:

1. Will the environmentalist *United Nations Biodiversity Treaty* force farmers and small property owners to abandon their homes and lands and "resettle" in approved government metro areas?

2. Does the Illuminati's Rockfeller Foundation now control the seeds of 95 percent of the Earth's major cereal crops— wheat, barley, and corn?

3. Is there a "Global Seeds Conspiracy" to place total ownership of the world's seeds—and ultimately the survival of mankind itself—in the hands of an elite cartel of multinational corporations?

4. Why are spy satellites now being used to monitor and control the crop production of farmers?

5. Are the police powers of the federal government—FBI, USDA, EPA, FDA, CIA, BATF, U.S. Fish and Wildlife Service, IRS, BLM, etc.—being used to taunt, harass, intimidate, frighten, impoverish, imprison and sometimes kill farmers, ranchers, and small land owners who oppose this Illuminati takeover of our food supply?

6. Are pre-planned and contrived "food shortages" on the way, with small farmers being purposely driven out of business? Will a starving and desperate American populace be left begging for federal government "saviors" to solve the crisis?

7. Is there an Illuminati plan for a powerful new United Nations agency, the *World Food Authority*, which will control the production and distribution of food?

8. In the coming deadly food shortages, who will be allowed the privilege of buying sufficient food to feed themselves... and who will be denied?

9. Should Christians and patriots immediately begin in earnest to acquire and store a year or more's supply of food?

10. Will anger and chaos soon grip the world as desperately hungry masses of people riot and storm grocery stores and supermarkets, only to find shelves cleaned out and empty?

11. What can you and I do now, before it is too late, to

prepare for the coming, severe food shortages? Is it possible that you, I, and our families can not only stay healthy, well fed, and safe, but also prosper during the coming hard times?

"The game plan is that a sudden shockwave of both hunger and financial misery hit America and the world. The resulting chaos will be carefully managed. The masses will be manipulated through brainwashing and government propaganda so that a New World Order (Novus Ordo Seclorum) may be established."

≈ 2 ≈

Famine and Pestilence
are Predetermined

Is an unparalleled crisis, bringing in its wake wide-scale hunger and starvation, foreordained for our immediate future? Is the resulting period of misery, turmoil, chaos and tribulation unavoidable? Are famine and pestilence predetermined?

To answer these momentous questions, we may profitably consult three primary sources. First, we can view past history. History has often served as a wise and reliable, if imperfect, indicator. As a keen historian once said, "He who fails to learn from the past is doomed to repeat it."

A second source is found in the area of contemporary conspiracy research. Documentation can be marshalled from the actual words, actions, and analysis of the hidden goals and purposes of the elite clique of super-rich bankers, financiers, and industrialists who own the great bulk of the world's financial and economic resources. As we'll discover, these same men also control the political destiny of the nations. However, the third source we will access is by far the most reliable and perfect. I refer here to the eye-opening prophecies contained in God's Holy Bible. In such gospels and books of the Bible as Daniel, Ezekiel, Zechariah, Matthew, and Revelation, we find astonishing predictions of dreadful, death-dealing famine and pestilence to occur in the last days just prior to Jesus' return.

Since every single prophecy that God's prophets have uttered and written down has come to pass now for some 3,000 years, we would be simple-minded fools not to consider what God has to say in His Word. And what the Bible prophesies for our future and that of our planet, Earth, is staggering, to say the least.

But first, let us see what the annals of history can reveal to us about the coming great hunger and what conspiratorial planners have in store for us on their drawing boards.

A Contrived Food Crisis?

Is there in existence a secret plan for a contrived food crisis? Many say this is an impossibility, that sinister plots and hidden conspiracies of such immense magnitude are creations of paranoid thinking. These skeptics often maintain that if such a secret plan, plot, or conspiracy existed, they would know about it. They insist they would have heard about it on TV or read about it in *Newsweek, USA Today* or in their local newspaper.

This is wishful thinking and sad ignorance on the part of the masses, who are always easily manipulated and deceived. Conspiracies and hidden schemes are rarely the stuff of your everyday newspaper or TV news reporting.

It is, nevertheless, an undeniable and easily proven

historical fact that secret conspiracies and elitist cabals have many times in the past artificially created famines, disease, epidemics, riots, assassinations, economic depressions, and mass chaos to attain their objectives. I have personally documented these facts in my many books, audiotape reports and newsletters.[1] Even the Encyclopedia Britannica and the various computer software editions of encyclopedias and historical reference books document the monstrous crimes of elitists who have conspired to terrorize, control, and starve their own populations. Stalin's forced collectivism during the 30s in the Soviet Union brought purging, torture, and death to tens of millions of Ukrainian and Russian farmers—and famine and hunger to tens of millions of city dwellers. And during the Nazi era, Hitler's minions severely rationed food to Jews in ghettos in Warsaw, Poland and other cities in Europe.

Mao Tse Tung's peasant army and his Red Guards enforced agricultural collectivism and brought a "cultural revolution" resulting in poverty, deprivation, and starvation to hundreds of millions of Chinese. Next door, in Cambodia, Pol Pot's Khmer Rouge Communists used regimentation and starvation as handy tools to wipe out up to one-third of the population of that once gentle nation.

These despicable crimes against humanity involving induced hunger and starvation have occurred in most of our lifetimes. But it is not only the Communists and Nazis who are guilty. The U.S. government used agent orange, a chemical defoliant, in Vietnam not only to clear out the dense, green foliage of giant jungles, but also to ravage farms and rice fields. One objective was deny food to the enemy. In the 60s and 70s, proprietary CIA aircraft flew missions over Fidel Castro's Cuba, aerially spraying that island nation's sugar cane and wheat fields with deadly chemicals and destroying Castro's primary source of foreign income. The same technology is often used in Mexico, Columbia, and other illegal drug-producing nations to defoliate and poison opium and marijuana plants.

Some Americans may rush to defend our government's

actions in places like Vietnam and Cuba as necessary to defeat or contain Communism. But even if such goals are worthy, the precedent is significant. This intentional poisoning by governments of agricultural crops and the destruction of farms brought marked success in producing mass hunger and famine. Such tactics have disrupted the enemy's economy and undermined his people's morale. Why would tyrannical governments now refrain from using such proven tactics against their own citizenry?

Ominous Experiments

In a very ominous and foreboding way, these early efforts to starve and control people served as experiments. They proved the adage prevalent today among the elite that, "Food is Power!"² Unfortunately, today's governments and the elite who run them behind-the-scenes have much greater, more refined, and more technologically sophisticated methods to induce famines and pestilence. Adolf, Joseph, Mao, and Pol would no doubt be proud and thrilled to have access to today's heinously efficient arsenals in government armories. Such methods include scientific tools such as weather modification techniques, electromagnetic anti-agriculture weapons, and ter-minator genes biologically produced to prevent seed reproduction. High tech means—satellites, video cameras, electronic tapes and monitors, computer databases, etc.—are also available to Big Brother governments for the enforcement of prohibitions applied to the agricultural sector and for monitoring of the movement and activities of the general population.

As if scientific and high tech means were not enough to reduce food supplies available to feed a hungry population, the United States government simply pays some farmers not to grow crops. In a later chapter, we'll examine this strategy as well as the federal government's funding, development and use of modern high tech methods to control populations and their food sources.

World Hunger to Usher in New Age Slavery

A hungry man or woman is a desperate man or woman. If a mother and father suffering hunger pains see their children also aching and debilitated from hunger, that adds all the more to their desperation. Maslow's hierarchy of needs demonstrates that if a person is physically hurting and hungry, that person cannot think of higher needs, such as the need for approval, self-esteem or intellectual stimulation. That would be a luxury. The afflicted person is, instead, consumed by the overwhelming desire to gratify his or her deprived appetite. The need for survival—and fear of pain and death— immediately takes precedence.

Add mob psychology to this primal need by individuals for survival, and you have a volatile mixture. The elite who control governments are well aware of this explosive mixture inherent in the hunger equation. They intend, therefore, to use it for their own gain and advantage.

The elite conspirators' objective is nothing less than to drive the people of the world's nations into a controlled and ordered spasm of desperate hunger so as to shepherd men into the feeding pen of global tyranny.

Thus, at a time and moment chosen by the elite, a hunger crisis of unthinkable proportions will be artificially created and thrust upon America and the nations. In their fearful wrestling with physical and emotional suffering and agony, the multitudes are expected to be willing do anything to have their survival problem fixed. Anything.

Chaos and The Plan

Believe me, when the teeming, starving masses cry out for food and for survival, the elitists, being masters of treachery and manipulation, are ready with a carefully prepared and orchestrated program of global, political, and economic domination. They have long had a "Plan," which they euphemistically call The Plan.[3] Lucis Trust President Mary

Bailey referred to the culmination of this "Divine Plan" as the opportunity that comes when unparalleled global crises arise. She wrote of "a tide in the affairs of men which can carry us on to the emergence of a New World Order."[4]

We must remember that the motto of the highest level, 33rd degree, of Freemasonry is the Latin phrase Ordo Ab Chao. The game plan is that a sudden shock wave of both hunger and financial misery hit America and the world. The resulting chaos will be carefully managed. The masses will be manipulated through media brainwashing and government propaganda so that a New World Order (Novus Ordo Seclorum) may be established.

Then, all nations, all races, all resources shall be consolidated and unified under centralized control. The plotters are New Age Utopians, Socialists, Marxists. Their objective is to synthesize, bring spiritually together, the nativism and Earth worship of the East with the last vestiges of a corrupt, jaded Western Christianity. There will also be the economic synthesis of Capitalism and Communism, proving incorrect Rudyard Kipling's famous maxim, "East is East and West is West and never the twain shall meet."

Interestingly, according to Jesuit scholar Malachi Martin, former distinguished professor of theology and church history at Georgetown University, the Catholic Church's Pope John Paul II is fully knowledgeable of the coming chaos and the goals of the elite.

The Pontiff is the spiritual leader for almost one billion Roman Catholics. In recent years, he has enjoyed the admiration and support of men who, in the distant past, would have been considered his Protestant foes—men like Billy Graham, Pat Robertson, Benny Hinn, Jerry Falwell, and Bill Bright.

Malachi Martin's remarks about the Pope are instructive since Martin is said to be an intimate confidant of the Pope and a close associate of influential members of the Vatican Curia, the highest inner circle of Catholic cardinals and other prelates. According to Martin, willing or not, ready or not, Pope John Paul II says that:

...by the end of this decade we will all live under the first One World Government that has existed in the society of nations...a government with absolute authority to declare the basic issues of human survival and human prosperity... our food supply...war, population control.[5]

The late Professor, Dr. Carrol Quigley, the mentor of President Bill Clinton, is yet another Georgetown University alumnus who possessed intimate knowledge of the The Plan. In his opus work *Tragedy and Hope: A History of the World in Our Time,* Quigley made this fascinating comment:

There does exist...an international network whose aim is to create a world system of financial control in private hands able to dominate the political system of each country and the economy of the world.[6]

A Universal Numbering System

Evidently, the Social Security system provides the networking conspirators the very tool they need to implement their tight system of human control because it requires, by law, that every person, from birth, be assigned a number for control purposes.

Previously the numbers were assigned only to workers. At the time of its inception, President Franklin D. Roosevelt (a 32nd degree Mason and an Illuminist) and the U.S. Congress promised that the Social Security number would never be used for "identification" purposes or for human control. They even reluctantly agreed to put this restriction into the law that created the system.

But the federal law enforcement bureaucracy and apparatus never did pay one bit of attention to that rather interesting and quaint little provision of the Social Security law. Thus, the government now maintains a gazillion files and dossiers identifying Americans by Social Security number. Only recently did Social Security numbers begin to be assigned to infants at birth. Meanwhile, Big Brother-style legislation passed in 1997, ostensibly to standardize drivers licenses in all 50 states, mandates that by the year 2000 each of the states require Social Security numbers of drivers license applicants as a means of computer control and identification.

By the dawning of the new millennium, every person's personal history, DNA, blood type, iris eye scan, fingerprint, etc., is to be tied in through his or her Social Security number to an international computer network known under the code word, L.U.C.I.D. I explored this Big Brother, human control project in my book, *Project L.U.C.I.D.*, noting that every nation on earth is now busy creating a numbering system for its populace and a computerized I.D. card system.[7] Eventually, rules and regulations will be promulgated so that no person on earth will be able to buy or sell food without their personal I.D. number.

This brings to pass Professor Carol Quigley's astonishing prediction that, in accordance with the plan and agenda of the global elite, "The individual's freedom and choice will be controlled from birth and followed as a number until your death."[8]

The Last Temptation of Antichrist

One especially insightful exposé book of the international machinations of the upper-level chieftains who have foisted on the world the New Age Movement is *Inside the New Age Nightmare*. The book's author, Randall Baer, a former New Age leader who converted to Christianity, warns that a supreme crisis is to be invented that will catapult the world into the willing and enthusiastic acceptance of the proffered New Order. Of the conspirators' plot, Baer writes:

> Their agenda is nothing less than the complete revolution-izing of the very foundation of not only America but the entire world. Such a plan calls for the total restructuring of planetary civilization into an enlightened One-World

Federation in which national boundaries and sovereignty are secondary, and "planetary citizenship" in the "global village" is the order of the day. This is to offer to a world in desperate need a grand solution to profound global problems. Apparent world peace and unprecedented opportunities for "actualizing the human god-potential" (i.e. New Age higher consciousness) are to be unveiled. Herein lies the Antichrist's last temptation, offered to all.[9]

The agenda of which Baer writes is the same as The Plan, which was conceived long ago in its essentials and which has been worked now for many decades. A number of famous and influential persons in numerous fields of human endeavor have been active in the 20th century to bring The Plan to fruition. For example, there was science fiction legend, British writer H.G. Wells, who worked diligently in his books to promote the New World Order. In his intriguing 1930s manuscript, *The Shape of Things to Come*, Wells postulates that when the future time comes that the World Government and the New World Order is ushered in by crisis, it will be seen that "It had been plainly coming for some years." Yet, writes H.G. Wells, "Although it had been endlessly feared and murmured against, it found no opposition prepared anywhere."[10]

This is chilling stuff. At a future moment of supreme world crisis, will those few of us who do have an inkling of The Plan and its agenda have our voices stilled by the duly appointed, jack-booted police of government bureaucracies— IRS, FBI, BATF, DEA, CIA, Mossad, Secret Service, etc.?

When the coming, great catastrophe of famine and pestilence—the most sensational crisis in human history— strikes planet Earth, will the masses discover that, suddenly, there can be "found no opposition prepared anywhere" to the proffered New World Order?

With the opposition stifled and overcome, the masses will have no alternative view of reality. There will be no truth presented them except the official version of truth. Frightened, with hunger pangs gnawing and tearing at their

innermost guts, the manipulated, sweaty, and frightened masses
are fully expected by the elite to cry out loudly and with one
uniform, wailing, and pleading voice:

> Please do something...anything. Save us! You are the wise
> men appointed over us. Do what is necessary. Just do it,
> and quick. We must have bread now, or we shall perish.

A Government Solution

In Imperial Rome, the decadent multitudes cried out for a
government solution. In answer, a decadent and morally corrupt
era of "bread and circuses" was initiated by the Caesars. The
government fed the people's appetite until the fall came. Then
the circuses ceased. This debauchery of the spirit made Rome
ripe for plunder and invasion by the barbarians. Then, Rome
descended into an intense period of suffering, hunger and death.

Likewise, in the 1930s in Germany, the multitudes cried
out for a government solution to runaway inflation, rampant
hunger and lawlessness. Hitler stepped forward to the beat of
martial music with his "solution" to their problems. Prosperity
ensued. The Fuhrer fed the peoples' appetites for awhile. Then
came the great disappointment, and the great fall.

In 1945, Hitler committed suicide. A surviving aide poured
kerosene on the corpse and burned the Fuhrer's body. Just
outside the bunker where Adolph Hitler's flesh was torched,
women and children in tattered clothes were ravaging in trash
cans and admist piles of rubble and garbage. They were
foraging for scraps of bread. Most had rejected Christ and
His truth and had, instead, sought and found a savior on
Earth. They were paying the consequences.

Is America Next?

Collectively, man has never learned the lessons of history.
Soon, the people of America will also be crying for relief.

The Illuminist elite already have prepared their solution to the clamor of the many Americans who will be roaming the streets and avenues, starving, begging and pleading for crumbs of food. The "Wise Men" who promise America and the world law and order, security, and a renewal of prosperity shall be warmly applauded as saviors.

However, though they promise a glittering New Age of prosperity and food in abundance, and though they pledge a program of restructuring and rebuilding, the brief ascendance of these evil men to absolute power will come to a most brutal end. As James, the brother of Jesus, so breathtakingly prophesied:

> Go to now, ye rich men, weep and howl for your miseries that shall come upon you. Your riches are corrupted, and your garments are moth eaten. Your gold and silver is cankered; and the rust of them shall be a witness against you. Ye have heaped treasure together for the last days. *(James 5:1-3)*

Destroy and Rebuild

With their objective of a new, colonialist society in mind, the arrogant god-men of the Illuminati will first destroy the world's economies, robbing men and women of their jobs, homes, and possessions. Then, they will deny to an impoverished and hurting humanity the basic food staples people need just to survive. Following their victory over subservient mens' wills, they will attempt to rebuild and recreate the world into a utopia of their own design and making.

As Reverend P. Huchedé, professor of theology at the Grand Seminary of Laval, France, wrote over 100 years ago in his classic book of predictions, *History of the Antichrist,* "It does not suffice to destroy. It is absolutely necessary to build up again."

From the debris and wreckage of the world's economies, the elite envision a restructured, global colonial empire. We shall all be slaves. They, our masters. Will their vision come true? What does the Bible say?

"And when he had opened the third seal, I heard the beast say, Come and see. And I beheld, and lo a black horse; and he that sat on him had a pair of balances in his hand. And I heard a voice in the midst of the four beasts say, A measure of wheat for a penny, and three measures of barley for a penny; and see thou hurt not the oil and the wine."

—Revelation 6:5-6

3

A Measure of Wheat, A Measure of Barley

Do you wish to view your future clearly, without impeded vision and with certainty? If so, what's necessary is that you and I turn to the one reliable source that is unimpeachable and unerringly correct: God's prophetic Word. The Holy Bible contains the story of man's history, from beginning to end, with the end told in advance. In this astounding book is found the destiny of the nations—and the destiny of you and I as individuals.

The fact is that God has already preordained the future, and His prophecies cannot be set aside. Though power-crazed men may plot to enrich themselves and may collude together to establish a New World Order, their unholy plans shall go awry. God confounds the best-laid schemes of His enemies. Thus, while the plots conceived in the fertile minds of wicked men should concern us, we know that their agenda can only come to pass if God wills it for his own ultimate purposes.

God, indeed, has a meticulously crafted plan—a Master Plan for mankind and for each man, woman, and child on this planet. It is important we examine that glorious and momentous plan. Therefore, we may profitably ask, what does God say in regard to the reality of a soon coming time of great hunger and economic despair?

The Four Horsemen of the Apocalypse

One of the most dramatic passages of scripture has to do with the Seven Seals in the book of *Revelation*. Only the Lamb (Jesus Christ) is accounted worthy to open the seals. In Revelation 6, we find the Lamb opening one of the seals. When He does, the mighty noise of thunder is heard, and the voice of one of the great creatures surrounding the Lord's throne in heaven says, *"Come and see."*

The Apostle John, to whom this stunning prophecy was revealed, saw in succession four horses. The first was a white horse,

> And he that sat on him had a bow; and a crown was given unto him: and he went forth conquering, and to conquer. *(Revelation 6:2)*

This rider of the white horse comes forth on the earth appearing to the deceived masses to be a messiah figure, a great ruler of nations. He holds out the false promise of global peace, but he is a conqueror who will ensure peace through strength and military superiority.

In our lifetime we have seen the emergence of this white horse and its rider. The United Nations, led by its mercenary forces—chiefly the armed might of the United States and its allies—has continually promised global peace to mankind. The U.S.A., sometimes acting alone as the world's superpower, but often launching military attacks on others in concert with its allies, constantly claims to be simply a democratic, peace-loving nation. But its imperialism, political and economic meddling, and messianic complex have marked America as a war-like power. The United States has waged war in dozens of countries, from Vietnam in Asia and Somalia in Africa to Cuba in the Caribbean.

The U.S.A. is not always at fault in these many wars and conflicts, but this great and powerful nation has presumed to act as the world's policeman and arbiter. As such, it has interfered in sovereign matters in capitals around the globe. Truly, it can be said that whether in Korea, Vietnam, Libya, Iraq, Somalia, Haiti, or Bosnia, the United States "went forth conquering, and to conquer."

Violence, however, begets violence, and the combined might of the United Nations/United States has not been able to fully stem the rising tide of barbarism and terror inflicted on innocents around the world. The New World Order cannot be sustained. Humpty-Dumpty cannot be put together again. Cracks surface and grow, and the intended global dictatorship is still, for the present, a mirage.

The Rider of the Red Horse

The rider of the white horse does not succeed in establishing his unified global kingdom. Peace is an illusion, for there will be no global peace until Jesus Christ comes again to set things right. Therefore, another horse, one even more war-like and bloody, is seen to come roaring onto the world scene:

> And there went another horse that was red: and power was given to him that sat thereon to take peace from the earth, and that they should kill one another: and there was given to him a great sword. *(Revelation 6:4)*

The rider of the white horse had a bow but no arrows. He preached peace but went forth to conquer to insure the peace. Peace, being afar off, is not possible to attain and thus comes the deadly sword wielded by the rider of the red horse. The color red signifies bloodshed and carnage. Peace having failed, men shall now "kill one another" with abandon, and the forces of evil shall be given the full means (*power*) to do their dirty work.

What to Do With Resisters

I believe the elite conspirators who are busy forging the New World Order are soon going to decide on massive force to be applied against those who oppose their planned global utopia. Nationalists, patriots, Christian fundamentalists, and other dissidents are already prominent on the elite's "Most Wanted" list. Already, the world's intelligence apparatus, its law enforcement agencies, and its armed forces are jointly tasked to identify, target, monitor, and, if necessary, wipe out all resistance to the agenda of the New World Order plotters.

Though the traditionalist patriots and Christian believers who know Bible prophecy are few in number, they have so far been amazingly adept in thwarting the ambitious schemes of the elite who rule this world behind the scenes. Rumblings of complaints are constantly heard from the lairs of the super-rich. They are angry because Christian and patriot dissenters to the New World Order so persuasively use the internet, shortwave radio, and alternative media (newsletters, word-of-mouth, etc.) to get out their truthful messages.

The conspirators feel that they must make an example of this pesky opposition. They also believe that once the few remaining dissenters are removed, the way will then be cleared for the sheep-like masses of the world to accept a total restructuring and revamping of society (*Perestroika*). All nations will be united into a Socialist/Fascist model (the synthesis of Communism and Capitalism).

The elite are convinced that the best way to proceed is

to unleash the dogs of war on the world. Even nations like America—that have historically enjoyed relative peace and tranquillity on their home soil—will be affected as the rider of the red horse, sword in hand, calmly goes about his bloody task of destruction and killing. The carnage, though global, will at first be limited and controlled. The limited purpose is to demolish opposition, but a greater purpose is to usher in conditions of financial misery, economic depression, and widespread hunger. Through inflicting mass pain, the elite expect to rebuild the fabled Tower of Babel, thus reconstructing the glories of ancient Mystery Babylon.

The Rider of the Black Horse

At this stage—and we are on the very threshold of it now— a contrived global hunger will descend like a dark cloud out of the sky. People who, a fortnight ago, were prosperous, well fed, and their lives filled with plenty, will suddenly find themselves out of work and their career and economic prospects dim. Worse, they will be shocked to find that even if they do have the financial resources and the money, there is almost no food available anywhere, at *any* price. This is the entry point, the laying of the foundation, for the *third rider* of the four horsemen of the apocalypse:

> And when he had opened the third seal, I heard the beast say, Come and see. And I beheld, and lo a black horse; and he that sat on him had a pair of balances in his hand. And I heard a voice in the midst of the four beasts say, A measure of wheat for a penny, and three measures of barley for a penny; and *see* thou hurt not the oil and the wine."
> *(Revelation 6:5-6)*

Note that the rider of the ominous black horse has a pair of balances in his hand, and he carefully measures out an allotment of food for the hungry—"A measure of wheat for a penny, and three measures of barley for a penny." The wheat and barley represent the world's grain supplies.

A Rationing of Food Supplies

We see, then, that food, though in short supply, will not necessarily be expensive. Evidently, the government will pass stiff laws and hastily issue executive orders that will curtail food hoarding and put a stop to price gouging. Otherwise, there would be a tremendous run-up in the price of foodstuffs and other commodities.

Essential food supplies will be carefully rationed from government-controlled warehouses and grocery distribution centers. Food will be made available at a cheap price in tiny quantities only to those who have a qualifying, government issued coupon or stamp. Obviously, there will be precious little food to go around.

The elite will, of course, be amply supplied with *all* their wants. They will live sumptuously. But the common people will be deprived of sufficient food even to sustain life. Starving fathers and mothers will resort to desperate acts to feed themselves and their families. They will steal and rob to acquire food coupons and stamps, but the government will put a stop to this rampaging thievery by instituting a computerized system of food rationing and issue. Thus shall be fulfilled the dreadful passage in Revelation 13:16-17:

> And he causeth all, both small and great, rich and poor, free and bond to receive a mark in their right hand, or in their foreheads: And that no man might buy or sell, save he that had the mark, or the name of the beast, or the number of his name.

The Mark of the Beast Will Be Resisted

At this point, however, things will get out of hand. The attempt by the governmental powers, under direct order of their hidden overlords—to cause all men either to take the mark, or else to suffer and die of starvation because they are unable to buy food—will not fully succeed. True, Bible-believing Christians, for example, knowing that all who take the mark, name, or number of the beast (*Revelation 13*) will be cast into the lake of fire when Jesus comes, will adamantly refuse. Many will be put to death. They will be beheaded for their faith.

God's anger and fury will be kindled at this heinous crime of massacre of his children on Earth. The carefully orchestrated plan of the elite will suddenly begin to come unraveled. Heaven's judgment will fall on their heads. Dissension will arise within their own ranks. Some within the hidden inner circle of Illuminati influence will revolt against their own leadership and attempt to seize the reigns of world political power. Assassinations, internal rebellions, and wars across national borders will spring up to plague humanity and prevent world peace. Terrorist attacks will multiply as one faction goes after another. Racism, ethnic hatreds, and national rivalries will explode. Civilians will be caught in the crossfire, and the forces of disruption and world war will bring universal devastation.

This last days warfare and factious squabbling will prove deadly. It will result in grisly death and suffering for hundreds of millions of people. Nuclear arms exploded will leave some cities and areas in tatters. Chemical-biological attacks will ensue as well. The combined effect of nuclear radiation and the employment of laser, chemical, and biological weapons will leave much of the earth denuded of vegetation. The assault will decimate any hopes of agricultural revival. *The acquisition of food will have become the principal occupation of individuals and families.*

Pale Horse to Bring Hunger and Death

No one will be safe from the invisible terror. In the case of biological attacks, once the odious organisms are released, the diseases spawned will rapidly spread. Fields of wheat, barley, corn and other grains and vegetables will be poisoned. Water supplies will be infected with toxins. One has only to consider the spread of the black death (bubonic plague) in Europe in the 14th century, an epidemic that left over 100 million dead—nearly half the population of that day.

The Bible prophesies that these dire events will occur immediately on the heels of the rider of the fourth and final horse, the frightening pale horse. When the rider of the pale horse comes, he will prove to be the consummate harbinger of death and starvation:

> And I looked, and behold a pale horse: and his name that sat on him was Death, and Hell followed with him. And power was given unto them over the fourth part of the earth, to kill with sword, and with hunger, and with death, and with the beasts of the earth. *(Revelation 6:8)*

The rider of the pale horse will usher in the slaughter by sword (war) and hunger of one-fourth the world's population. In our present world of six billion inhabitants, that means the destruction of 1,500,000,000 men, women, and children! When the bible says that "Hell followed with him," surely this is no exaggeration.

Famine, Pestilence, and Thirst to Ravage and Kill

People will not be able to trust and rely on either their meager quantities of food or their life-giving water supply. In Revelation 16:3, we see that an angel will cast his vial upon the seas, leaving the oceans ruined and extinguishing fish and all other forms of sea life.

Ezekiel, the Old Testament prophet, envisioned just such a day, when people would be frightened even to eat and drink: "Son of man, eat thy bread with quaking, and drink thy water with trembling and with carefulness." (Ezekiel 12:18)

City dwellers, especially, will be plagued, said the prophet:

"He that is in the city, famine and pestilence shall devour him." (Ezekiel 7:15)

There are two good reasons why Ezekiel's prophetic words will soon be translated into unpleasant reality. First, cities are prime targets for radioactive nuclear warheads. Second, in the throes of inhumane world war, teams of terrorists and saboteurs can be expected to detonate high-level radiation charges and deposit chemical-biological agents in waterways. The result will be the breaking out of dreadful epidemics and widespread sickness as the poisoned water is drunk by people and cattle and used to water agricultural fields.

Ezekiel painted a haunting image of a time of grim, future ruination of water supplies by terrorists when he pointed out that people would "drink their water with astonishment... because of the violence of all them that dwell therein." (Ezekiel 12:19)

Cannibalism to Plague Mankind

The prophets say that men will die from hunger, and some will become so desperate that they will mutilate themselves in seeking to satisfy their all-consuming hunger:

> And he shall snatch on the right hand, and be hungry;
> and he shall eat on the left hand, and they shall not be
> satisfied: they shall eat every man the flesh of his own
> arm. *(Isaiah 9:20)*

Others, driven to murderous acts and sacrilege by lack of food, will turn to the flesh of their fellowmen as the world of the last days devolves into a frantic struggle for survival: "That that dieth, let it die... and let the rest eat every one the flesh of another." (Zechariah 11:9)

Let us not rationalize that these ghastly prophecies are warnings of symbolic events, or that they are dramatizations. When we consider the depraved acts that have historically occurred when men and women were deprived of food and water, we realize the literal truth of the prophecies. Survivors of ships lost at sea and survivors of crashed aircraft have, in desperation, indeed eaten human flesh in their determined but ghastly quest to stay alive. During the siege and destruction of Jerusalem by the Roman General Titus in 70 AD, historians record that some Jewish women literally killed and ate their own babies!

In the *Appendix*, I examine the utter devastation that can be caused by invisible agents of death—chemical and biological weapons, nuclear bomb explosions and radiation fallout, weather modification technology, and earthquake-inducing methods. All of these are tools available to technologically advanced governments, either to be employed clandestinely against selected populations on a limited scale in theater conflicts, or in general, all-out war.

That these weapons and other, more mundane, methods will be employed is sure. Our Lord Jesus Himself prophesied that in the latter stages of time, *"There shall be famines and pestilences and earthquakes in divers places."* (Matthew 24:7)

Hunger will surely stalk America and the seven continents of the planet in days soon to come. These things will occur *before* Jesus' return. In their wake, scriptures reveal to us that the faithful in the Lord, the Church, will be lifted up from the Earth. Then, the terrible judgment of God will fall upon the remaining inhabitants of Earth (Isaiah 26-27). Men's hearts will fail them so great will be the terror of those days.

Men will try to hide themselves in caves knowing that the great day of His wrath has come:

> And the kings of the earth, and the great men, and the
> rich men, and the chief captains, and the mighty men, and
> every bondman, and every free man, hid themselves in the
> dens and in the rocks of the mountains; And said to the
> mountains and rocks, Fall on us, and hide us from the
> face of him that sitteth on the throne, and from the wrath
> of the Lamb: For the great day of his wrath is come; and
> who shall be able to stand? *(Revelation 6:15-17)*

The High and Mighty to Fall

The coming famine and pestilence are predetermined. Powerful, cruelly sinful men will be used by demonic forces as instruments to bring God's prophecies to pass. Unsaved, suffering men, their expectations of prosperity or even basic survival dashed, will curse their circumstances. Eventually, the high and mighty among them—whose power-mad actions caused this great calamity to befall mankind—will themselves fall victim to disease, hunger and physical suffering and death.

As occurred in the French Revolution and the Soviet purges, the tormentors will become the tormented. The killers shall, in turn, be slain by their own devices. In bloody France, the evil Robespierre, who grinned at and taunted those whom he sent to the guillotine, was eventually himself led to the guillotine and beheaded. In Russia, the ruthless secret police chief, Beria, eagerly sent his own associates to gulags and to firing squads. Then, he, too, was arrested and shot.

Having oppressed the downtrodden and brought hunger to the masses in expectation of gaining even greater wealth and power, the elite schemers will eventually discover that what they sow, they shall also reap. They shall be consumed by pestilence (disease), by hunger, and by death.

The wisdom of Job, himself beset with terrible tribulation, sagely instructs us on the end result for the super-rich elite and their human followers who reject God, and who unmercifully prey on the poor and mock the righteous. Their New World Order triumph shall be short-lived, indeed:

> Knowest thou not this of old since man was placed upon the earth. That the triumphing of the wicked is short... Though his excellency mount up to the heavens, and his head reach into the clouds. Yet he shall perish forever... *(Job 20:4-7)*

> Because he hath oppressed and hath forsaken the poor; because he hath violently taken away an house which he

builded not; Surely he shall not feel quietness in his
belly...*(Job 20:19-20)*

There shall be none of his meat be left... When he is
about to fill his belly, God shall cast the fury of His wrath
upon him, and shall rain it upon him while he is eating."
(Job 20:21, 23)

Good News for Believers

Jesus said there would finally be an end to the horrors:

And except those days should be shortened, there should
no flesh be saved: but for the elect's sake those days shall
be shortened. *(Matthew 24:22)*

Herein lies the key to protection and survival for the
Christian believer. God does not bring wrath upon His own.
It is true that wicked men, inspired by the Adversary, do
plot our death and visit tribulation and hardship upon us.
Believers are not immune from hard times. Yet, in the very
midst of a universal era of misery and despair, God's people
will find contentment and optimism in the future.

It is a wonderful thing that the people of God do not fear
and quake in time of crisis and disaster. Those who know
God fear only Him. In times of urgent need, He is their
deliverance. As Christians, we do not fear the coming great
hunger nor the tragedies that shall accompany it. Miraculously,
God will keep us secure no matter what the enemy may do:

Behold, the eye of the Lord *is* upon them that fear him,
upon them that hope in his mercy; to deliver their soul
from death, and to keep them alive in famine. Our soul
waiteth for the Lord: he *is* our help and our shield. For
our heart shall rejoice in him, because we have trusted in
his holy name. Let thy mercy, O Lord, be upon us,
according as we hope in thee. *(Psalms 33:18-22)*

God uses the works of evildoers and the ravages of nature to magnify His name and bring Him glory. The story of Elijah in the Bible is instructive. God regularly fed him by way of a bird bringing him food in a time of famine. In Egypt, Joseph was given the interpretation of a vision of seven years of famine to come. The Pharaoh believed God's man and prepared the nation. While many starved, Egypt lived and prospered.

> The Lord knoweth the days of the upright: and their inheritance shall be forever. They shall not be ashamed in the evil time: and in the days of famine they shall be satisfied. *(Psalms 37:18-19)*

King David of Israel tells us in Psalms:

> I have been young, and *now* am old; yet have I not seen the righteous forsaken, nor his seed begging bread. *(Psalms 37:25)*

> But the salvation of the righteous *is* of the Lord: *he is* their strength in the time of trouble. And the Lord help them, and deliver them: he shall deliver them from the wicked, and save them, because they trust in him. *(Psalms 37:39-40)*

Do you trust in the Lord? Is He your strength? It is, of course, the right thing to do all we can in our human strength to prepare for the coming hard times. We can store up food and water, and fortify our homes to keep out would-be thieves, burglars, and rioters. We can acquire firearms sufficient to defend ourselves from angry, crazed, and hungry looters when things really begin to grow dark and ugly.

But ultimately, our reliance on our own strength can never be enough. Without God, we are doomed. *With God, all things are possible.*

"We're continuing to have our spy satellites in the sky, they're there to help us. What we're doing is mapping and monitoring the entire world, including every square inch of the United States..."

—Vice President Albert Gore

❦ 4 ❦

Big Brother is Watching
Our Food Supplies

B
ig brother is closely watching and monitoring our food supplies. To paraphrase a grand, old Christmas tune, "He's making a list, checking it twice. Gonna find out who's naughty or nice..."

In the *Omega Times*, a Christian newspaper published in New Zealand, my good friend, Barry Smith, warned of the plans of Big Brother to create the prophesied end-times dictatorship based on control of food. He noted that small farmers are being driven out of the market and that, "flat farm land that was previously stocked with contented cows munching on green grass is no more."[1]

Smith, in his article, reminded readers of the ominous statement once attributed to Henry Kissinger at a secretive

Bilderbergers meeting in Europe. Kissinger, former U.S. Secretary of State and now an active Rockefeller foreign affairs operative, declared: "By controlling energy we can control nations, and by controlling food we can control individuals."

Kissinger and associates are succeeding, said Smith, warning that, "The result is obvious—less food worldwide and the fulfillment of the Biblical scenario of a worldwide famine."[2]

Also in the same issue of *Omega Times*, Barry Smith stated: "Not only are New Zealand farmers under attack, but this attack is reaching out into Europe."[3]

The London Daily Telegraph certainly confirmed the situation in Europe when the highly regarded newspaper reported:

> *Farmers Made to Watch Crops Rot.* Farmers are being forced to let hundred of acres of early ripening vegetables rot because they are forbidden by European Union rules from picking them. Under European rules, to insure that farmers cannot claim subsidies for set aside land and then grow crops for profit on that same land, they are not allowed to harvest vegetables until after January 15.[4]

The Same London newspaper observed that similar controls on farmers are in place in the United States:

> During a trip to the United States two years ago, we asked a farmer why he was not planting food in a certain field. And the answer given was that, "He was not allowed to," as the Federal Agricultural Authorities had made it quite clear there was a limit put on farmers as to how much food they were allowed to sow at any certain time of the year."[5]

Government Tells Farmers What to Plant

Some time ago, some thirty years ago, a good friend of mine in the U.S. Air Force announced his pending retirement, and I said, "What are you going to do now that you are getting out of the Air Force?" My good friend, Sergeant Jim Bagwell, answered, "Well, I'll tell ya, I'm going to be a farmer. I'm going to be a peanut farmer. I'm going back to Oklahoma."

"That's great, Jim" I responded. "Do you have a piece of land picked out?"

"Well," he said, "It's complicated; you see, you can buy one piece of land and it can cost a thousand dollars an acre. But a piece of land sitting right next to it is worth only fifty dollars an acre. I want the land that costs a thousand dollars an acre."

I raised my eyebrows and said, "Well, that sounds foolish." And he said, "No, it's not, there are only certain pieces of land that got a quota from the government way back in the 1930s that can even grow peanuts. Not everyone can grow peanuts."

"What do you mean?" I asked, "Anyone can go out and buy a thousand acres of land and plant peanuts if he wants to. It's your land, and you can do what you want with it."

"No, you can't," said Jim. "The federal government tells you what you can plant and what you can't plant of certain commodities, and peanuts is one."

Being young and naive at the time, I was flabbergasted. In America? Farmers told they *cannot* plant and sell a crop? Incredible! I had no idea the government could tell a person who owns land that he can't use it to plant what he wants. And if he does use it, he can't sell the products. But the government does have the authority, and they have been exercising this unconstitutional authority in America for some sixty years. And, of course, by now we know of the Environmental Protection Agency, the Bureau of Land Management and all of the other federal environmental groups. They're busy day after day telling people, you can't plant this and you can't plant that. You can't farm here and you can't farm there. If you farm on your land, they're saying, and you harm a certain beetle—or a bug, a rat or a snake—that's endangered, we will put you in jail because you're an enviro-criminal.

Don't think they're not doing it. I have an entire list of men and women, farmers and other citizens who are in prison today because they decided to go ahead and plow their fields or use their land—*their own land.* They owned it, they thought. Now, according to the Fifth Amendment of the Bill of Rights to our Constitution, the government cannot take your land or property without due process, and the government must pay just compensation. Even then, they can only acquire private land or property for a legitimate government purpose. That's a legal principle called *Eminent Domain.*

Whether they want to construct a recreational park, a federal highway, a library, or a youth center on it, if the government wants your land, they are required by the Constitution to go through a process of *Eminent Domain* and pay you just compensation.

Regrettably, today, the federal government simply disregards due process. And the federal courts do not obey the Constitution of the United States of America. And they have not been obeying it for many years now.

Are Maniacs Running the World?

But why are governments in New Zealand, Australia, Europe, and the United States so determined to *reduce* the available food supply by making it unlawful to plant crops? Why are farmers ordered to sit idly by and watch crops rot in the field? We've all seen the photographs of the starving, emaciated children in famine-stricken Ethiopia. We've seen, too, the dying babies in Somalia and Bangladesh with distended stomachs, gaunt, hollow cheeks, and dull, vacuous eyes.

What kind of maniacs are running this world to pay some farmers *not* to grow crops and to threaten others with imprisonment if they harvest healthy crops, while millions of men, women, and children literally starve to death?

Big Brother is alive and well, it seems. And when the food crunch comes for us here in America, Big Brother, most assuredly, will continue to pass and enforce irrational and insane laws and regulations intended to starve people into submission.

Lawrence Patterson, astute publisher of *Criminal Politics* magazine, makes the ironic point that, in the event of a contrived food crisis, governmental authorities may well take steps to cut off food supplies and to confiscate food from citizens who have "too much" on hand:

> Americans should be investigating one other very important item, stored food. As I have pointed out, the New World Order and its people may eventually block the interstates and cut off deliveries of food into the cities. It might be that they will be searching for food, for arms, and for ammunition. They will want to see if you are hoarding food. If you've got too much food, they'll decide you don't need so much.[6]

High tech inventory systems make feasible the most minute monitoring of food distribution. Because of computers, everything you buy now is monitored and duly recorded. We have the laser scanner, the bar code reader.

The media have already unfairly painted a picture of certain groups as evil and dangerous. Christians and patriots are frequently bashed and lied about. Are you buying more food than the government may think you need for your family? Someday, the authorities might just start keeping a tab on it. Are you one of those despised Christian fundamentalists or one of those feared militia types that are actually storing food? As soon as the big food shortage begins to bear down, the authorities will use computers and other high tech systems to enforce rationing and quotas.

When the Oklahoma City bombing occurred in 1993, I read a national news column by some idiotic liberal reporter who said, "It's time that we start rationing and controlling the supply of fertilizer." When the crisis hits and terrorist attacks occur, if you've got a lawn and you've gone down to your local food store, or nursery lawn store and bought a fifty pound bag of fertilizer to make your lawn more green or to help your garden grow, you might have to show identification or present a ration card. Fertilizer will be controlled. The government and media will point out that bomber Timothy McVey used fertilizer to make his bomb used to demolish the federal building in Oklahoma City.

The Treaty From Hell

The government is adept in using crises and chaos for control. We have the United Nations Biodiversity Treaty awaiting passage, a pact I call the "Treaty From Hell." President Bill Clinton signed it, it's been held up in the United States Senate, but the White House is already implementing its draconian provisions. The treaty will, upon full implementation, force farmers and small landowners literally to abandon their homes and resettle in approved government encampments of "communities" adjacent to, or in, metropolitan areas.

An essential part of the United Nations Biodiversity Treaty is the setting up of international biospheres. These are regions, territories, or geographic areas of the country in which the land must be left pristine and untouched by humans. Also being implemented now by the U.S. government is the *Wildlands Project*—the rewilding of America. That, we are told, will insure protection of Mother Earth and preservation of the habitat of endangered species. Only in certain enclaves will people be permitted to live. Eventually, up to ninety percent of all U.S. land will be returned to a wild state. Tens of thousands of farmers will be forcibly removed and evicted from their rural farms and homes as a result of the Biodiversity Treaty and the Wildlands Project.

Two of the stated objectives of the UN's Biodiversity Treaty are:

1. To make man equal to other species; and

2. To create large geographic areas devoid of human presence.[7]

Humans are to be considered strictly as a "biological resource," no more important to the ecosystem than a roach, a snake, or an ant. In any case, people, after all, are in plentiful supply. By evicting the people from most of America's lands and turning these rewilded lands over to the United Nations' World Environmental Authority, the objective of creating huge, interconnected wilderness areas devoid of human presence will be achieved.

Some cities and urban areas which are claimed to be precious environmental resources may also be denuded of people. A city like Memphis, Tennessee, they may say, has a certain kind of endangered lizard, and so everyone in Memphis, Tennessee will have to move out, abandon their homes, and resettle in an approved area.

Resettlement and Pacification

You say, "That can't happen in America." Friends, I can show you that down in Central America during the guerilla wars, we, the United States, through the Central Intelligence Agency, carried out planned programs to resettle the people, the peasants. We did the same thing in Vietnam. In Vietnam the U.S. government called it the Pacification Program, and policy-makers said that to pacify the people, we would (and did!) force entire villages to fold up. The inhabitants had to tread out with their belongings, and live behind barbed wire under conditions remarkably similar to concentration camps. We did it to the Japanese here in the United States during World War II. And let me tell you, the CIA still has in its computers the data necessary to reinstitute the "Operation Phoenix" assassination program and the pacification methods used in Vietnam. They have also programmed into CIA computers the methods used in the Central American resettlement process in Nicaragua.

This same crime against people and property has been perpetrated on people by dictators all over the world. In Cambodia, the *Khmer Rouge* Communists did it. They actually closed up the capital city of Phnom Penh in Cambodia. The city had a population of well over one million people. At gunpoint, the Communists forced everyone out of the city and told them they had to resettle somewhere else in the countryside. Well, there were people who couldn't move; for example, bedridden patients in hospitals. The armed agents of Communist dictator Pol Pot simply blew their heads off, and they died, left in their beds to rot.

Some elderly people didn't want to leave their homes. They too, were killed—shot or bludgeoned to death by the inhumane *Khmer Rouge* troops. Resettlement, it was called. And now we have the United Nations Biodiversity Treaty. And the demons who possessed Pol Pot's savage soldiers and bureaucrats have possessed and are now working through today's Big Brother federal government, its environmentalist allies, and the United Nations.

Big Brother and Corporations in Bed Together

Big Brother is also in bed with corporate giants and wealthy dynasties such as the Rockefellers and the Rothschilds. Did you know that the Illuminati's Rockefeller Foundation and other groups controlled by the Rockefellers now control the seeds of ninety-five percent of the earth's cereal crops— wheat, barley and corn? Is there, in fact, a global seed conspiracy that places total ownership of the world's seeds and ultimately the survival of mankind itself in the hands of an elite cartel of multinational corporations? And even if they didn't control the seeds, through their agribusiness corporations, today they own most of the farming land, as well as the means of distribution.

What if in the last days a farmer were to say, "I'm going to go out, plant and then harvest my crops and I'm going to sell to Christians who can't buy from a retail food store or shop because they don't want to take the mark of the beast. I'll plant my food crops and I will secretly get food to these brave Christian people."

Well, he's going to have to ship his food by rail, by truck, or by boat. What if all of those distribution methods are owned and monitored by the cartel, the elite clique that controls the New World Order?

The Seed Conspiracy

However, it is the seed conspiracy that gives the elite the most control. If you're going to dominate the food supply, what would you start with? I'd start with the seeds, wouldn't you? If a farmer is not going to get the seeds, he's not going to produce crops. You can control other factors, too. You can manipulate the debt system and buy up most of the farms, driving the small farmers out of business and setting up your own agricultural cartel. You can own the huge grain silos and the railroads and the means of distribution and, therefore, control the food. You can buy up the huge supermarket chains and control the direct sale of food to customers. But if you want to get *total control* at the most essential, basic level, just start with the seeds.

Many years ago people stored seeds from their crops and the next year they used the seeds, and they would keep going that way, year after year. Not anymore. Multinational corporations, in their research labs, developed new hybrid seeds. And they went to the farmers and said, "Would you like to get a greater yield from your crops? Then don't use your own traditional seeds for tomatoes, beans, wheat, and rice; use our seeds; buy *our* seeds—they're far better and produce greater yields per acre."

Farmers did it, and over the years—especially the last fifteen to twenty years as farmers used these hybrid seeds—it has turned out that many farmers no longer have seeds of their own.

At the same time, the large multinational corporations of the cartel that controls the food in the world obtained patents on hybrid seeds. You cannot simply use the seed from one year's crops for succeeding crops because they own the patent on the seeds. That is labeled theft of private property. You must go back to the seed corporation each year for the seeds. We can imagine the problems this can cause. What happens if you need seeds for your next crop and there are no seeds? And they say, "Oh, we're sorry, a problem occurred in our warehouses, vermin got it, or some kind of new blight on seeds, some kind of virus is affecting the seeds, we can't give them to you." Imagine the incredible food shortages that would soon occur.

Well, here's what the Abundant Life Seed Foundation said in its newsletter, *Seed Midan*, about the stark reality that today confronts farmers who are dependent on others for their seeds:

> Patenting issues are encroaching on our lives in pervasive ways. Small farmers have lost their right to sell and save patented seed. Heirloom seeds that have been in families for generations are disappearing, and large corporations are owning the sole right to these seeds. Chemical and pharmaceutical corporations stand to make hundreds of millions and even billions of dollars from the control and commercialization of biological resources and patents for seeds. For example, this has resulted in:
>
> 1. Farmers being denied their traditional right to save seeds.
>
> 2. Farmers being forced to pay royalties for every seed and for animals derived from patented stock. There are better pigs, better cows, and the means to feed them and the drugs that are used, and the types of cows that you see through genetic engineering, bioengineering, they're developing better stock. But once you buy into it and start using their better stock, and you have to in order to compete or they'll put you out of business, after all if they have more yield, if they have fatter stock than yours, you'll be driven out of business. So, you're forced to use their

patented products, and then they control you through the patent process.

3. Farmers are becoming more dependent on herbicides and fertilizers made by the same companies who collected their traditional seeds in the first place and now sell back the chemically dependent varieties.[8]

The Rockefeller Foundation and the seed cartel are ingenious. They have developed and maintained a seed bank which retains a sizeable quantity of the traditional seeds. Yes, they retained those seeds and stored them. Their corporations built storage rooms that keep out the weather, the air and the moisture, to retain the vitality of these seeds. They have the traditional seeds, but they're not going to give them to the farmer because they want him to buy their new, expensive hybrid seed products. This is how they control the farmer.

Amazingly, while most Americans slept, seeds were altered in corporate laboratories, and now we're told that those companies own the patents and have the intellectual property rights to those genetic plant materials because they have improved them.

What was once viewed as the farmer's inalienable right— the ten thousand year old ritual of saving seed from a harvested crop—has been jeopardized by plant patent laws at the national and international levels.

I received a letter from a ministry friend from Tennessee not too long ago; he wrote:

Dear Texe...The one thing that they (the conspiracy) got control of is our food. Yet, this has never been mentioned by the media or newspapers. By hybridizing, farmers stopped saving their seeds from year to year. So now, the pure, original seeds are no longer available. When the crash comes, there will not be any crop seeds. Where is the food? I can see millions starving due to no ability to grow crops.

Some of you may say, "Well, I won't depend on the farmers. I'll just start growing my own crop in my own back yard." The question is, who will give *you* the seed to plant your garden?

Genetic Colonialism

In *Time* magazine there was an article entitled *Seeds of Conflict.* It stated: "Critics say a U.S. company's patent on a pesticide from an Indian tree is genetic colonialism."[9]

You see, there is a little tree grown in India called the Indian kneem tree. Well, W.R. Grace & Company (you might remember that the late J. Peter Grace was head of the North American division of the Knights of Malta, the Vatican secret society), a huge chemical and ship-building corporation very closely involved in New World Order happenings, patented a pesticide made from the seeds of the Indian kneem tree. The W.R. Grace Corporation is telling the people of India they can no longer make a home-produced pesticide from this tree because W.R. Grace owns the patent on the seeds. So, in effect, this corporation claims to own the tree.

You might think that farmers in India would just tell W.R. Grace, a multinational company, to get lost, to jump in the lake. Not so, because India is a member of the World Trade Organization (WTO). The WTO consistently can be expected to side with the corporate cartel against the interests of native farmers.

The WTO, an international body, was set up not by *treaty* but by *trade agreement* with the United States. This illegally bypassed the Constitutional requirement that treaties must be approved with consent of the U.S. Senate. Instead, Congress simply passed a legislative act and pretended that an "agreement" with over 150 nations around the globe was not technically a "treaty." So America's trade policies now are under the authority of the World Trade Organization. America is a member of the WTO just like we are part of the United Nations. The WTO polices and enforces trade and commerce for almost every nation on Ea th. America is thus stripped of its sovereignty in these matters. The same is true for India, and that country's natural resources are being plundered.

Survival of Mankind in Jeopardy?

Recently, in a magazine called *Nexus*, in an in-depth article entitled *Seeds: Survival or Ser itude*, Ken Corbitt asks, "Is there a global seed conspiracy? Have the multinational seed corporations already sown our future?" Answering, he proclaimed: "Total control of the world's seeds and ultimately the survival of mankind itself is now in the hands of an elite cartel of multinational corporations."[10]

Corbitt also reported:

> Governments worldwide must comply with the demands of the seed monopolies. If they do not, officials and individuals can receive six months jail time and fines of $250,000 for breaching patents or breaching royalties.

> Global Biodiversity is under grave threat. Since 1970, as genetically engineered seeds tolerant to herbicides, with designer genes and primed profit, replaced heritage seeds, multinationals have acquired 1,000 seed and plant breeding companies. In the 1980s alone, they invested a staggering $10 billion dollars on seed company acquisitions.

> The multinationals have absolute control over not only the initial seed varieties but any derived plants, plus all transgenic and hybrid varieties they can produce. The patent laws will demand royalties from growers while the seed companies have ultimate power over mankind. Control over what we eat, when we eat, or if we eat at all.[11]

The Rockefeller Foundation, often linked to the New World Order, provided $90 million dollars to researchers in the decades of the 30s, 40s, and 50s. This money was used to fund research in molecular biology, which is the basis of genetic engineering. The Rockefeller Foundation's press releases claimed they were helping the poor farmer down South. Some skeptics, however, believe that the trustees had a more malevolent objective in mind. They had their sights set on a multibillion grab of the food supplies of the world.

The same Rockefeller Foundation has collected the traditional seeds of ninety-five percent of the earth's major cereal crops of wheat, barley, and corn. One expert has said, "This is nothing less than DNA, Inc."[12]

While the world's traditional, heritage seeds are stored away by the cartel in frozen gene banks, the natural varieties are slowly being phased out by farmers. While farmers have done this out of necessity, to remain competitive, this has left the farmers reliant on expensive, hybridized seed that now cannot regrow viable seeds. The newer varieties of crops also require large amounts of chemicals and herbicides, which farmers are required to purchase. Many farmers in Australia have been hauled before the courts, accused of growing or replanting seeds not on the national list of approved species. Did you get that? There is now a list of "approved species."

The United Nations and Seed Control

Meanwhile, the United Nations is steadily strengthening its powers in the area of food production. There is a United Nations directorate called the World Food and Agricultural Organization (WFAO). It wants to turn itself into a World Food Authority (WFA). We have the World Trade Organization (WTO). The elite and liberal churchmen are pushing for a United Religious Organization (URO), and just recently, an International Criminal Court (ICC) was established. Soon, we're going to have a World Food Authority. Undoubtedly, this WFA organization will be empowered to tell farmers what they can and cannot grow. If its bureaucrats find you are growing something that is not on their approved list, you'll be in trouble because you don't own the rights to the seeds. Planting these patented seeds without permission could be a criminal offense. They'll want to know how you got the seeds.

You've heard of *gun control*, well, now there is *seed control*.

Spies in the Sky

How could they accomplish such a thing? How could they police this? If you've got land, how will the government even know *what* you're planting? Let me relate to you something very interesting. *The European* newspaper recently printed an eye-opening news item headlined, "*Spies in Sky Zero in on Farm Cheats.*" Here's what the news article reported:

> Brussels has launched spy satellite surveillance of Europe's nine million farmers in the intensifying war on fraud. In all but two of the twelve states of Europe, the fields of thousands of farmers who make bogus claims for hefty government subsidies are being detected with pinpoint accuracy.

> For the first time, satellite surveillance makes it possible to carry out checks on virtually every farm. Largely superseding the cumbersome procedure of random, on-the-spot checks by agricultural ministry officials.

> In Brussels, Belgium, the commission is collating the spy satellite data, then passing it on to national enforcement agencies in readiness for a blitz against farmer fraudsters once the autumn harvest begins.[13]

In the United States, according to news reports, Congress was shocked to discover that the *National Reconnaissance Office (NRO),* an agency affiliated with the super-sleuth high tech agency, the National Security Agency, and the Central Intelligence Agency, had built a new office building just outside

Spy satellites are now used by Europe and the United States to monitor farmers' fields and insure farmers are complying with production quotas, environmental regulations, and the blizzard of new laws being passed to restrict and control farming activities.

of the Washington, D.C., beltway. The building cost a staggering $350 million dollars. It had been built in secret. Spy agency officials had put a fake name on the building site during construction, and no one knew.

Finally, a few members of Congress who had inquiring minds wanted to know about the gargantuan building that was going up. They were stunned when they discovered its purpose was to house the National Reconnaissance Office. This agency is made up of thousands of Intelligence agents and technology bureaucrats who analyze and evaluate the data, images, and pictures that come from spy satellites in the sky.

Now, you may be very curious that with the end of the Cold War we still have all of these surveillance satellites in the sky. Supposedly, Russia is now our friend. Right? The Soviet threat during the Cold War was the pretext that was used to develop spy satellite system. What are we still doing with all these spy satellites, and what are we doing with a gigantic building, costing taxpayers 350 million dollars, housing a mysterious, little known National Reconnaissance Office (NRO)?

The answer soon came from Vice President Al Gore, who made a speech, reported in the national press, designed to throw people off a bit in their suspicions. Gore said:

> We're continuing to have our spy satellites in the sky; they're there to help us. What we're doing is mapping and monitoring the entire world, including every square inch of the United States, and we're looking for environmental problems. We're studying the world and its surface for environmental problems.[14]

According to my sources, we now have the capability, through sophisticated photographic cameras operated from these spy satellites and platforms, to survey the entire Earth. So detailed are the images that these cameras are able to detect the logo printed on a golf ball sitting on the green of a golf course. Imagine, a spy satellite can now read the letters of your auto's license plate. Satellites high in the sky you cannot even see can make a picture of you. Later, technical analysts, photo in hand, can determine whether you're bald-headed, whether you wear glasses, what color your hair is, how tall you are, what kind of car you're driving, or what you're planting in your back yard or on your farm lands. They can count how many livestock you have in your fields. The NRO's spy eyes in the sky have the means to minutely control you.

Al Gore assures us: "We're going to use all of the spy satellites, and all of the reconnaissance capability we had before in fighting the Cold War and use it to save our Earth and monitor the environment."[15]

If you believe that, my friends, I have a bridge I'd like to sell you going across a swamp in Louisiana. We're already seen in *The European* newspaper that the European Union government is concerned that some farmers are planting more than they're supposed to. These farmers have quotas, and they're accused of cheating. Spy satellites acquire images, their computers calculate and know exactly where the land is that the illegal crop is being grown on, and they report this data to the authorities. The farmer is arrested, fined, and possibly taken to jail. He's a criminal for using his land.

It's a very scary thing when we begin to see these kind of things happening. It is also tragic to think that America's dumbed-down citizens will be duped into believing that satellite spying of our farm lands is necessary to protect the environment or to save endangered species.

The Hills Have Eyes

In *Nature Conservancy* magazine, published and distributed by one of the nation's most radical eco-propaganda groups, was a recent article with the arresting title, "The Hills Have Eyes."[16] It reported how the Nature Conservancy, a Rockefeller and elite funded organization, is working closely with the U.S. Army at Fort Hood, Texas, employing Landsat satellites, computers, and infrared video cameras to watch, track, and monitor birds. At least they *claim* it is "birds" that they are watching. Read these key paragraphs from the article, and you'll grasp the frightening potential that government and antihuman groups like the Nature Conservancy now have to intrude on our privacy and nose into peoples' private business:

> Dusk, June 30, 1997. Fort Hood in Central Texas. Grainy images flicker across the screen. Through the lens of the surveillance camera, figures periodically enter and exit the scene. Though the picture is black-and-white, the camera's infrared light illuminates the evening with an eerie glow. Motion provides context, and we begin to understand what we are spying on: a pair of birds feeding their nestlings...

Video is just one monitoring device in a high tech toolbox Nature Conservancy scientists are using to try to save the black-capped vireo and another songbird, the golden-cheeked warbler, from extinction. Other tools—satellite imagery, global positioning systems and radio telemetry—amount to kinds of "eyes" watching these birds, whether from a nest or from space.[17]

What the *Nature Conservancy* magazine failed to tell its readers were the facts about the vicious war the U.S. Fish and Wildlife Service and their fanatical, environmental associates are waging against farmers and ranchers in Central Texas. They are lodging mostly fictitious claims that ranching and farming is harmful to the birds' habitat ("habitat" is claimed to include almost the entire Texas hill country—tens of thousands of acres of lands and cities and towns with a combined population of about three million people!). Unfortunately, the environmentalists and their government thug pals have been able to bring use of much of this land to a virtual standstill.

Individual land owners in Texas are being told by the feds that if they cut down one cedar tree or use their own land productively for anything (for a barn, a shed, or a home, for example), they will be criminals and will be prosecuted to the full extent of the law. Thousands of acres are being abandoned, ranchers and farmers have gone bankrupt, and environmental wackos win again.

Someday, these same environmental activists will wonder what happened to their food supplies. For now, they are helping the government to develop a satellite/video spy system to watch and monitor the habitat of birds. Is it really the birds they are protecting or is it their multinational corporation benefactors who are profiting? After all, the corporations seek to limit and control the production of farm commodities and beef market products. By taking tens of thousands of acres off production rolls, food commodities grow scarce. Food supplies are steadily diminishing, thanks to the outrageous land grab of the environmentalist organizations, federal bureaucrats, and their monied cohorts who operate the food cartel.

Watching All of North America

As more and more farmers and private property owners have come to understand what is really going on, the conspirators have sought new ways to hide their dirty work. I recently came across an article in *Machine Design* magazine which tried to convince farmers of just how wonderful satellite spy systems can be. The article, claiming that, "satellite mapping reaps higher crop yields," glowingly reported that farmers can use satellite technology to keep track of crop moisture, productivity volume, and other data. It stated that, thanks to a new GPS satellite orbited by a company named Omnistar, positioning signals are being mapped "over all crop-growing regions in Northern America."[18] The satellites are able to monitor a farmer's field within a few feet of its boundaries.

Splendid, huh? Big Brother is, indeed, watching over our food supplies.

Meanwhile, the world's richest corporation, Microsoft, has announced its new *TerraServer* web site on the global internet. It seems that Microsoft's chairman, multibillionaire computer software magnate Bill Gates, has created the biggest database in the world. TerraServer's web site contains satellite images covering almost the entire globe, down to one meter's resolution. Microsoft says that the images are from the U.S. Geological Survey (photos provided by National Reconnaissance Office satellites) and the Russian Space Agency. Online web users, including environmentalist activists and police state agencies, will be able to search the web site and zoom in to any spot on earth—even peer into *your* back yard!

Is it a coincidence that Bill Gates regularly attends former Soviet Communist dictator Mikhail Gorbachev's annual State of the World Forum in San Francisco? Is it a coincidence that Gorbachev is head of the International Green Cross, one of the world's premier anti-small farmer and anti-small rancher environmentalist groups? Is it a coincidence that, in a recent television interview, Microsoft's Bill Gates, the world's richest man, admitted that, like Gorbachev, he does not believe in a personal God?

A Grave Threat to Our Future

It is for sure that spy satellite technology represents a grave threat to our future. *Revelation 13* prophesies that a commercial system will be set up so that, in the last days, no person will be able to buy or sell food or any other product unless he or she has the mark of the beast, or his name, or the number of his name—666. When that momentous time of testing comes, the government authorities will not allow you to barter for food. They will pass and enforce laws that require you to obtain food only from approved sources. Undoubtedly, unless you take the name, mark or number in your forehead or in your hand, you'll not be permitted to grow your own garden, because you will not be able to buy hybrid seeds—the only seeds marketed.

With their spy satellites, the authorities will make sure you can't grow what you're not supposed to. You can't grow watermelons, you can't grow corn, you can't grow tomatoes, because you don't have the seeds; they control the seeds, the patents on the seeds. And therefore, if you plant tomatoes in your back yard and a spy satellite discovers your crime and reports you to the local police, you will be arrested—just like men and women are now arrested for planting illegal marijuana plants.

America's prisons are today full to capacity with convicts found guilty of the production, distribution, and use of illegal drug substances. Someday, more prisons will have to be built, even concentration camps used, to house the legions of convicts incarcerated as "food criminals."

> "And the Earth brought forth vegetation, the herb yielding seed after its kind, and the tree yielding fruit, whose seed was in itself, after its kind. And God saw that it was good."
>
> —Genesis 1:12

> "The Terminator Technology is brilliant science and arguably 'good business.' But it has crossed the line between genius and insanity. It is a dangerous, bad idea that should be banned."
>
> —Geri Guidetti
> The Ark Institute

⚘ 5 ⚘

Demon Seeds—The Seed Conspiracy and the Terminator Gene

If a cabal of cunning and ruthless rich men wanted to take over the world, how would they do it? Napoleon and Hitler sought conquest through nationalistic jingoism and military might, and failed miserably. Lenin, Stalin, and Mao tried the economic ideology of Communism, state bureaucracies, and the employment of brutal secret police against the people—also a colossal failure.

How would you, as a tiny cadre, or cabal, of influential world powerbrokers proceed given the fact that so many in the past have had their expectations thoroughly dashed and their once expansive empires crushed, broken or dissolved?

This has, for decades, been the question haunting the ambitious men who comprise the inner circle of the global Illuminati. But now, finally, thanks to the astounding scientific miracles of modern technology, the cabal of globalist conspirators whom I named and unmasked in my classic book, *Circle of Intrigue,* have discovered an amazing formula which, they believe, will crown with success their aspirations for world dictatorship.

The chief conspirators are in unanimous agreement: The ages-old quest for domination of the human species is soon to culminate in victory—the Holy Grail has been discovered. The Illuminati now understand that the path to New Age mastery over the six billion assorted individuals who populate planet Earth is found in their *bellies.* The elite now realize that if they can but control men's food for survival, then access to their hearts and minds will surely follow.

And the best way—indeed, the only *real* way—to control men's access to food is to establish hegemony at the most basic starting point, at the very beginning: the *seed.*

Thus, we are now confronted with what can only be described as the most diabolically ingenious of all conspiracies. Involving the quest to totally subvert the cherished possession of all freedom and liberty for humanity—this is the *Seed Conspiracy.*

The life sciences of genetic engineering and agricultural hybrid technology have combined to provide our world controllers with the exact ingredients needed to fuel their greedy lust for money and for power over all human beings. The scientists have now developed what has been called the *"demon seed."* Very few Americans have even the most scant information of, or knowledge about, this demon seed. Before too many years, they will know—but it will be too late.

Rise of the Terminator Gene

"Ever since there has been agriculture, farmers have saved their seeds from this year's crop to replant for next year's," explains Jim Hightower, former Commissioner of Agriculture for the State of Texas. "Not just economic sense," Hightower says, "this is also an ecological boon, because so many farmers saving so many seeds helps strengthen local strains and promotes a broad genetic diversity in the world's crops. Selecting, saving, and exchanging seeds with neighbors is just smart agriculture."[1]

But now, Hightower wryly adds, along comes the federal government, in collusion with multinational corporations, to dramatically transform the whole landscape of seeds, the farms, and their crops. The scientists of the United States Department of Agriculture, working hand-in-glove with the scientists of corporate laboratories, have developed the amazing *Terminator Gene*.

The terminator gene is a bioengineered element that mutates a seed's genetic structure rendering the seed barren and unable to reproduce itself. The changed seed will produce a product—say corn, rice, wheat, or barley. It just won't reproduce itself.

Here's the bottom line: The corporations own the patent to the hybrid, genetically engineered seed. The seed has a built-in *"terminator gene."* It produces one time only. Thus, after a farmer's crop is harvested and sent to market there are no seeds left behind to be stored, exchanged, or used for next year's crop. The farmer will have to go after each and every harvest to the supplier of the seeds—the multinational corporation—and buy his seeds for the next crop. Farmers will have become merely the planter of someone else's "good for one crop only" seeds. In effect, the old Southern-style farming system that kept poor blacks and whites alike in bondage is revived. Farmers are increasingly becoming *sharecroppers.* In European countries it used to be called *serfs,* or *peasants.*

It is important we take a look at what some expert analysts

are saying about the terminator gene and the new hybrid, nonreproducible seed.

Fat Profits for Corporations

In *The European* newspaper (roughly equivalent to our *USA Today*), Cath Blackledge, in a two part series entitled, *The Green Revolution,* asked the question, "Will terminator seeds bear fat profits?" Blackledge's conclusions are quite revealing. With the terminator seed, what Blackledge calls "Life sciences" firms will make astonishing sums of money by controlling the whole food chain. Here's some of what Blackledge reported:

> Monsanto, the world's leading agricultural biotechnology company, has a new product: the terminator seed. This seed, which is likely to be commercialized in the next five years, is unlike all previous seeds. Farmers who plant it are in for a surprise. The terminator seed cannot be replanted...

> On offer to the farmer is the following bargain: buy the new seeds and benefit from a new generation of genetically-engineered crops offering high yields and resistance to disease. But in return, go back to the seed company every year to buy new seed, rather than replanting stockpiled or harvested seed.

> The terminator seed is at the cutting edge of an agricultural revolution, led by Monsanto, which is seeking to gain a foothold in Europe after sweeping through America...

> Monsanto is positioning themselves to make money from this revolution by effectively controlling the whole food chain, from the seed to the dinner table...

> Three years ago Monsanto acquired a new chief executive, Robert Shapiro, and a new focus: agricultural biotechnology.

Since then, the St. Louis giant has been on a spending spree, splashing out $6.7 billion on a string of seed and biotechnology firms, including Calgene, producer of the world's first genetically-engineered tomato, the flavr savr. Two weeks ago it spent roughly $4.2 billion on swallowing the 60 percent of biotechnology seeds firm DeKalb Genetics it didn't already own and snapping up the stock of America's largest producer of cotton seed, Delta & Pine Land (co-creator, with America's Department of Agriculture, of the terminator technology).

Last week, it said it plans to work with the world's third largest food company, Cargill, to link seeds through processing to the customer.

More acquisitions are expected. Two years ago it planted its first batch of genetically-engineered seeds; this year it expects to harvest approximately 20 million hectares of genetically-engineered crops worldwide.

Monsanto is not the only firm suddenly to find agricultural biotechnology sexy. The majority of life sciences groups— the new breed of company which has shifted its focus from chemicals to human, plant and animal health—are fighting to snap up seed and biotechnology companies in the hope that they will bear fat profits.

DowElanco (a joint Dow and Eli Lilly venture) is trying to buy the 31 percent of seed firm Mycogen it doesn't own, ahead of its agreed purchase date of February 1999. DuPont, under its new chief executive, Charles Holliday, is following in Monsanto's footsteps: it is to spin off its oil and gas business, Conoco, and spend the proceeds on life sciences acquisitions, adding to its $3 billion spent on agricultural biotechnology last year.

Europe's companies are not being left out. Ciba and Sandoz's merger created Europe's leading life sciences

firm, Plant Genetic Systems. It wants to buy the rest.
Zeneca went Dutch, linking its seeds arm with that of the
Dutch firm, Suiker Unie, to create Advanta and buying a
Leiden-based plant biotechnology firm, Mogen, last year.

The battle is worth fighting: the global food production
market is worth $400 billion...

The control of the food chain and food production by a
handful of firms in order to reap huge profits is what the
stampede to buy into agricultural biotechnology is all
about. But snapping up seeds companies is unlikely to
satisfy life sciences giants for long. Linking up with a
like-minded company could be next on the list for
Monsanto. Who knows? Next century may see its
completing and controlling the food chain with a
collaboration with one of the major food processing firms.
This is the Green Revolution—but this time it's about
control of more than feeding the world: it's also about
what we eat and how we live our lives.[2]

The Coke and Pepsi of Crops

The prestigious *The Wall Street Journal* has also kept up
with this fantastic race to reap giant profits by controlling
the food chain. In a feature article on biotech crops, Scott
Kilman and Susan Warren showed insight with their comments:

Monsanto Co. and DuPont Co. are betting the farm in bids
to transform themselves into the Coke and Pepsi of
genetically engineered crops.

In the three years since the first transgenic seeds were
introduced, crop biotechnology has grown from a young
science to a hot business: About half of U.S. cotton
fields, 40% of soybean fields and 20% of corn fields this
year are genetically altered. Now, in a stunningly swift

concentration of power, much of the design, harvest, and processing of genetically engineered crops is coming under these two companies' influence.

Not long ago, Monsanto, of St. Louis and DuPont, of Wilmington, Del., were chemical companies slugging it out over synthetic carpet fibers. Now, they are spending billions of dollars on talent, technology and other biotechnology assets, racing to rewire the nation's crop of corn, soybeans and other mainstays for use in everything from new types of food to pharmaceuticals and plastic.

Over the last 12 months, the two companies have been escalating their war on several fronts. There has already been a price battle over the genetically engineered seed sold to farmers, and their bidding contests for seed companies are pushing prices into the stratosphere.

They are racing to build "dirt-to-dinner" biotechnology pipelines, with enormous implications for the nation's food supply. And many agriculture officials and academics are already leery of their rapid growth. "What's happening is mind-boggling," says Marshall Martin, a Purdue University expert on biotechnology public policy. "The worry out there is that this is becoming an oligopolistic situation."

In recent weeks, Monsanto and DuPont have pulled into their competing camps many of the most important plant-biotechnology assets, including seed producers. Seeds are the bridge between biotech labs and the nation's farmers, the delivery mechanism for the genes that scientists cook up.

Through direct investment and alliances, the two rivals are getting control of seed producers for most major U.S. crops. Combined, they would control roughly half of the U.S. seed market for soybeans and even more of the seed market for corn—the nation's two largest crops. Monsanto alone stands to control a staggering 80% of the U.S.

cottonseed market, if pending transactions win regulatory approval.

DuPont is spending $1.7 billion on a joint venture with the nation's biggest seed producer, Pioneer Hi-Bred International. Monsanto, already the owner of established seed lines such as Asgrow and Holden's, now has agreements to buy DeKalb Genetics Corp., the # 2 U.S. seed company, and Delta & Pine Land Co., the giant cottonseed company. Monsanto's tab over the past two years for these deals stands to be $6.7 billion.

Eventually, DuPont hopes to be able to take orders for a new type of crop from food companies such as Nestle SA or ConAgra Inc., create it in the laboratory, contract farmers to grow millions of acres, and process it into a food ingredient. DuPont agreed to pay $2.6 billion to buy out its partner, Merck & Co., in a pharmaceuticals venture, giving DuPont control and allowing it to speed research into plants capable of making drugs as well as healthier food.

Monsanto is catching up by forming a joint venture with grain-processing behemoth Cargill Inc. The venture will use Cargill's sprawling system of rural grain elevators to contract with farmers to grow genetically engineered crops and mill them into ingredients. They would sell the ingredients to Cargill's customers...

In the first wave of biotech crops—plants designed to resist insects and exposure to powerful weedkillers— Monsanto is far ahead. Seeds equipped with Monsanto genes are being planted around the globe this year on roughly 55 million acres—roughly the size of all the farmland in Iowa and Illinois...

Wall Street is so infatuated with crop biotechnology that analysts are dreaming up scenarios for DuPont and

Monsanto to get together. A combination between the two is a persistent and intriguing rumor.[3]

A Global Seeds Conspiracy?

However, it is not just Monsanto and DuPont that are working furiously to grab hold of market dominance in seeds. A number of cartel firms are involved. One of the most insightful investigations into what is happening was an article by Ken Corbitt, published in *Nexus* magazine, entitled *"Seeds: Survival or Servitude?"* Corbitt held back no punches. This, he warns, is nothing less than a "Global Seeds Conspiracy!"

According to Corbitt, less than 20 major corporations, including W.R. Grace, Bayer, Pfizer, Monsanto, now control global seed supplies. They dominate in the U.S.A., Brazil, Australia, Thailand, Great Britain, France, Hungary, Egypt, and the Ukraine—in fact, in almost every nation on Earth. Corbitt reports that:

> Total control of the world's seeds—and ultimately the survival of mankind itself—is now in the hands of an elite cartel of multinational corporations. Complicitious governments worldwide are enacting Plant Breeders' Rights legislation to enforce the seed monopolies, with six-month jail terms and fines of $250,000 for breaching patents or not paying royalties.
>
> Global biodiversity is under grave threat as genetically-engineered seeds—tolerant to herbicides, 'designer-gened' and primed for profits—replace heritage seeds.
>
> "Seed-saver" networks and conservationists in many nations are fighting a grassroots action to protect natural and regional plant varieties from extinction and to alert the world to the threat of control of the world's food supply, genetic manipulation, and laws that will allow the process patenting of all plants, animals, fungi, genes and viruses.

The world seeds market will be worth many billions by the
year 2000, yet only a handful of major players—mainly
petro-agri-chemical multinationals—will reap the rewards.

Less than 20 major corporations now control global seed
supplies; many are seeking patents on any newly-developed
hybrids or those produced by transgenics (genetic
engineering, or GE).

Multinationals have acquired 1,000 seed and plant-breeding
companies since 1970; in the 1980s alone they invested a
staggering US$10 billion on company acquisitions...

Intense lobbying by the seeds cartel at the Uruguay Round
of negotiations of the UN General Agreement on Tariffs
and Trade (GATT) paid off: countries under the
International Convention for the Protection of New
Varieties (UPOV) are enacting Plant Breeders' Rights
(PBR) bills and launching them on unsuspecting
communities around the world.

Academics and civil libertarians have condemned the bills
and the awarding of process patent rights that offer the
multinationals absolute control over not only initial seed
varieties but any derived plants, plus all transgenic and
hybrid varieties they can produce.

The patent laws will demand royalties from growers, while
the seed companies have the ultimate power over mankind:
Control over what we eat, when we eat—or if we eat at all.

Australian scientist Richard Hindmarsh believes
biotechnology and plant-breeders' rights in the hands of a
corrupt corporate-state monopoly is the recipe for a 'Brave
New World' of genetic manipulation, and corporate
enclosure of the DNA commons.

He says that the so-called 'Green Revolution' of the late

1960s/70s was a ploy not only to make the Third World reliant on agrichemicals and hybridized seed, but to "steal" as many plant varieties as possible for their patented seed banks.

And the new power-push for breeders' rights and seeds control is just another item on the agenda to world domination. The facts bear this out: the Rockefeller Foundation, often linked to the New World Order, provided US$90 million to fund research into molecular biology, the basis of genetic engineering from the 1930s to 1959. It helps fund the Philippines-based International Rice Research Institute (IRRI), which is still suffering its Green Revolution failures—as are the farmers. The same Rockefeller Foundation also collected the seeds of 95 percent of the earth's major cereal crops—wheat, barley, and corn—in the years leading up to the GATT treaty and Plant Breeders' Rights bills.

So while the world's seeds are stored in frozen gene banks, the natural varieties in the Third World countries can be slowly "phased out," leaving the farmers reliant on expensive, hybridized seed that can't re-grow viable seeds, requires large amounts of chemicals, and ultimately sends the small farmers broke.

As Richard Hindmarsh sees it: "It's just another tool of DNA Incorporated."[4]

A Clear and Present Danger

Consider again Ken Corbitt's warning that multinational corporations, colluding with governments, will have "the ultimate power over mankind: Control over what we eat, when we eat, or if we eat at all."

The implications are, indeed, staggering. Geri Guidetti of the ARK Institute, a group founded to alert the public to this clear and present danger to their food and their freedom states, "There have been times in human history when the line between genius and insanity was so fine that it was barely perceptible. In the world of biotechnology and food, that line has just been obliterated."[5]

Guidetti says that the frightening situation seems to have developed almost overnight, coming into clarity after several startling announcements by major pharmaceutical, chemical, oil, and agribusiness firms of their intentions regarding use of the terminator gene and other high tech, hybridization techniques:

An ingenuous scientific achievement and subsequent, related business developments threaten to terminate the natural, God-given right and ability of people everywhere to freely grow food to feed themselves and others. Never before has man created such an insidiously dangerous, far-reaching and potentially "perfect" plan to control the livelihoods, food supply, and even survival of all humans on the planet. Overstatement? Judge for yourself.

On March 3, 1998, the U.S. Department of Agriculture (USDA) and the Delta and Pine Land Company, a Mississippi firm and the largest cotton seed company in the world, announced that they had jointly developed and received a patent (US patent number 5,723,765) on a new agricultural biotechnology. Benignly titled, "Control of Plant Gene Expression," the new patent will permit its owners and licensees to create sterile seed by cleverly and selectively programming a plant's DNA to kill its own embryos. The patent applies to plants and seeds of all species.

Pea pods, tomatoes, peppers, heads of wheat and ears of corn will essentially become seed morgues. In one broad, brazen stroke of his hand, man will have irretrievably broken the plant-to-seed-to-plant-to seed-cycle, THE cycle that supports most life on the planet. No seed, no food—unless—unless you buy more seed. This is obviously good for seed companies. As it turns out, it is also good for the

US Department of Agriculture....The USDA and Delta & Pine Land Co. have applied for patents on the terminator technology in at least 78 countries!

Once the technology is commercialized, the USDA will earn royalties of about 5% of net sales. "I think it will be profitable for USDA," USDA spokesman Phelps said. (Royalties? Profits? For a Department of the US Federal Government? What's wrong with this picture?)[6]

Geri Guidetti's remarks on how fast this has all come about are very significant and bear repeating: " In one broad, brazen stroke of his hand, man will have irretrievably broken the plant-to-seed-to-plant-to-seed cycle, THE cycle that supports most life on the planet. No seed, no food—unless—you buy more seed."

New World Order Creates "Bioserfdom"

Jeff Baker, author of *Cheque Mate: The Game of Princes,* a book exposing the global conspiracy of government and money, suggests that the control of agricultural production and food supply is a fulfillment of Bible prophecy:

This will allow the complete control of all food-growing in the hands of a few New World Order (NWO) companies, creating, as one writer put it, "bioserfdom." Remember friends, the NWO folks believe that, "food is power," and they will use it to change behavior, so that no man may buy or sell, save he that had the mark of the beast."[7]

If there are those who would doubt my claim in *Days of Hunger, Days of Chaos* that the federal government and the multinational corporate elite are colluding together to pull off the biggest heist in human history—the monopolistic grab of seeds and food—this is convincing proof that what I report is accurate. Scientists of the U.S. Department of Agriculture

(USDA) worked side-by-side with Delta and Pine Land Company, itself owned by a chemical conglomerate, to develop the new Terminator Gene technology. Now, the USDA and the corporation co-own the patent, and the federal government will get to keep five percent of net sales. That's untold billions of dollars annually in profits.

The government to actually make a profit? Sounds unbelievable. But consider the big picture: Isn't it Socialism, or a variant of Fascism, when Capitalist enterprises and government bureaucracies co-own property? Isn't it a striking precedent, indeed, when taxpayers' monies are used by the government to create or invent marketable products and then share those patent rights with preferred corporations?

The significance of this is enormous. Will the U.S. government soon co-own the patent rights to the entire range of seeds? In fact, the USDA does have other crops in its biotech sights, including maize, corn, and rice.

Edward Hammond, program officer of the Rural Advancement Foundation International, states. "We find it particularly bothersome and disturbing that it was the U.S. Department of Agriculture that developed the technology."[8]

What is mind-boggling is that the government and the seed cartel are taking existing seeds, already in use and given to us naturally by nature (God!), and genetically altering these older, reliable, conventional seed strains. The claim is that the altered seeds are more hardy, disease resistant, produce more yield, and in some cases, have technologically bred into them the capability to perform complex pharmaceutical tasks. Once corporate/government researchers have patented the improved seed, they are claiming ownership of whole species of food plants—on the logic that, having altered a gene in a member of that species, they now own the whole genome.

A Matter of Food Security

Geri Guidetti and the Ark Institute are worried that the introduction of the Terminator Gene in all plant species could seriously threaten food security for every person on Earth:

> I have often fretted about the vulnerabilities of our increasingly centralized, computer-based, bottom-line driven, large corporation-dominated, food production, processing and distribution system. Extreme weather patterns, toxic waste-contaminated fertilizers, epidemic bacterial contamination of food, and the year 2000 crash of computers responsible for keeping the whole, complex system running have been big concerns. I have warned of the planned disappearance of non-hybrid, open pollinated seeds—seeds that let you retain the means of growing your own food if you want or need to—seeds that ensure protective biodiversity—seeds that may provide personal food security in insecure times. Now the Terminator threatens even these.[9]

Guidetti's conclusions are sobering.

> Make no mistake about it—widespread global adoption of the newly patented Terminator Technology will ensure absolute dependence of farmers, and the people they feed, on multinational corporations for their seed and food. Dependence does not foster freedom. On the contrary, dependence fosters a loss of freedom. Dependence does not increase personal power, it diminishes it. When you are dependent, you relinquish control. History is full of examples of peoples and cultures who lost fundamental freedoms—who were controlled—by their need for food.[10]

The Rural Advancement Foundation International (RAFI), a nonprofit group established to boost and encourage small farms, believes that the "Terminator Technology" could prove more disastrous than the much talked about Y2K computer bug glitch. The RAFI contends that, "The 12,000 year old practice of farm families saving their best seed from one years' harvest for the next season may be coming to an end." RAFI goes on to warn:

By the year 2000, farmers may no longer be able to save seed or breed improved variations. The problem is not the Millennium Bug but the "Millennium Seed."[11]

Camila Montecinas, of the Center for Education and Technology, in Chile, accuses the multinational corporations of having a "greed gene." The patenting and licensing of seeds, says Montecinas, means that "1.4 billion farm families are at risk."[12]

True, small farmers can continue to use older varieties of seeds—unpatented varieties—for planting. But they will be at a tremendous disadvantage in doing so. In any event, very soon, certainly by the year 2005 if not sooner, the seed cartel and the food processing and distribution cartel will have merged market forces. Farmers will be told that the crops grown from the older, natural seeds can no longer be marketed. The cartel will refuse to buy the traditionally produced crops. Farmers will then have two choices: either buy the new, nonreproducible Terminator Gene seeds, perhaps at exorbitant prices, or go out of business.

Seeds, Power and Mischief

It is easy to see that control of seeds translates effectively to *power*—power over the farmer, power over what we eat, power over how much is available to eat, and power over what our food will cost.

Even Jim Hightower, former Secretary of Agriculture for the State of Texas and usually a liberal who loves Big Government interference in almost every aspect of our lives, is taken aback by the potential mischief of the Terminator Gene. On the internet recently, Hightower complained about the U.S. Department of Agriculture "playing kissy-face with the giants of agribusiness which keep finding new ways to mess with Mother Nature for their own fun and profit.'"[13]

"In their latest scheme," writes Hightower, "government scientists and corporate profiteers have teamed up to mess up one of nature's basics: seeds." Hightower brands the new hybrids "barren seeds" and goes on to observe that, Ever since there has been agriculture, farmers have saved their seeds from this year's crop to replant next years....So along come the geniuses at USDA, using our tax dollars to develop a seed that will not germinate when replanted....Who would want such non-germinating seeds? The seed corporations, of course, since it means every farmer in the world would have to come to them and buy new seeds."[14]

Hightower asks the pertinent question, why is a government agency, the U.S. Department of Agriculture, involved in this scenario? And he uncovers the revealing, if troubling, answer:

> "The world's farmers and the genetic diversity of our food supply are in danger of being terminated. So why did USDA pursue it? The goal, according to an agency spokesman is "to increase the value of proprietary seeds owned by U.S. seed companies."

> This is Jim Hightower saying....Silly me, I thought USDA's goal was to serve the needs of consumers and farmers, not to increase the profits of agribusiness corporations."[15]

Frankenstein and The Demon Seed

Could the introduction of unnatural, lab-invented genes into natural plants cause problems? Could, somehow, nature itself be harmed? Could the whole array of plants and crops throughout nature be neutered and—either inadvertently or on purpose—be destroyed? If so, then science may be planting seeds of human destruction.

Today, in an almost Frankensteinian manner, plants are being mated with genes of hogs, scorpions, even of humans, resulting in hybrid species of strange dimensions.

The Economist, an establishment magazine of economic business and finance published jointly in a number of world capitals, printed a fascinating article, entitled, *"In Defense of the Demon Seed."* The magazine's editors favor the new strains of seeds and food plants being created in laboratories. but they did add one, rather unusual cautionary note:

...Dangerous and mysterious forces are plainly at work.... One concern is the idea that...laboratory modification introduces alien and unnatural genes into crops...where their eventual effects are unknown...Does it make sense to meddle with nature for the sake of a sweeter beet or a brighter tomato?[16]

The magazine argued that public concerns that plants grown from modified seeds could unexpectedly strip the planet of all life are unfounded and not based on scientific study. However, critics point out that once these Terminator Gene plants are out in open fields, bees and other insects will cross-pollinate them with wild trees and plants. Disastrously, all of nature's plants will then naturally mutate for themselves into varieties containing hybridized Terminator Genes.

The changes in plant chemistry, affecting every plant on Earth, are unknown. Even *The Economist* admits: "If something goes wrong, how can it be put right? The truth is, nobody knows."

Imagine the green things of the world—all plant life— suddenly vanishing, killed off by a spreading and mutating Terminator Gene. This would mean the death by starvation of much of humanity—a tragedy of biblical proportions. Indeed, mass death on this type of cataclysmic scale is exactly what is prophesied in the Holy Bible!

Demon seeds may just turn out to be designer monstrosities that pollute and disrupt our food supply and terminally upset the very balance of nature.

Interfering With God's Natural Order

How significant, therefore, are the warnings given in our Holy Bible that man is not to interfere with God's natural

"In Defense of the Demon Seed" was the feature article in this issue of **The Economist,** an influential establishment magazine published in London and sold in the U.S.A. and throughout the world. The writer of the revealing article admitted that introducing the Terminator Gene into agricultural seeds and crops could lead to dangerous, unforeseen consequences. However, the magazine endorsed the new technology as a potential money-maker for multinational corporations with potentially significant benefits for humanity. Why, then, did the magazine choose for its article title the eye-opening provocative phrase, **demon seed?**

order in regard to seeds and life? In his thoughtful *Intelligence Newsletter,* New Mexico Pastor Earl Jones says that God is adamantly against this scientific process. Jones points to the Old Testament book of Deuteronomy 22:9 where we are given the commandment: "Thou shalt not sow thy vineyard with divers seeds: lest the fruit of thy seed which thou hast sown, and the fruit of thy vineyard, be defiled."[17]

In Leviticus 19:19 we also find: "Ye shall keep my statutes, thou shalt not let thy cattle gender with a diverse kind: thou shalt not sow thy field with mingled seed: neither shall a garment mingled of linen and woollen come upon thee."

Is man and his science more intelligent than God? Jones' answer is—"no!" He writes: "God doesn't want his animals hybridized. He doesn't want his crops hybridized...Have you ever noticed that some hybrid seeds will not reproduce at all, and some will reproduce in some grotesque way?"[18]

I agree with Pastor Jones' concerns about man's tampering with nature for profit in developing this dangerous new hybrid. Does not the word "grotesque" ably describe the profound implications of the Frankenstein, Terminator Gene seeds?

Should we not heed the Scriptures? It was at the beginning that God created the *natural* process of breeding and selection. No mixing of pig and human hybrid genes. No corn and scorpion hybrid (these are actually being genetically engineered today). God's original plan was that each seed, each tree, each fruit, be brought forth after its kind:

"And the Earth brought forth vegetation, the herb yielding seed after its kind, and the tree yielding seed after its kind. And God saw that it was good." (*Genesis* 1:12)

> *"The majority of Americans have no earthly idea that regardless of how bountiful a harvest farmers may have, a famine may, at any moment, be artificially created by a small clique of powerful conglomerates. All that's necessary is for the cartel to give the order and the food distribution system grinds to a crunching halt."*

❦ 6 ❦

Global Cartel Controls and Manipulates World Food Supplies

"**N**o one knows how they operate, what their profits are, what they pay in taxes and what effect they have on foreign policy— or much of anything else about them." These were the words of Senator Frank Church (D-Idaho), Chairman of a U.S. Senate Committee investigating the six international conglomerates that control America's and the entire world's grain production, and its meat packing and distribution. Senator Church, a determined opponent of the elitist oligarchy, made the statement in 1975, but the same facts hold true today.

In 1986, Rudy "Butch" Stanko, in his book, *The Score,* identified the world grain and commodities cartel as being composed of such international giants as Con-Agra, Dreyfus,

Continental, Bunge, and Andre. Stanko, who says his $20 million meat packing company was harassed and finally bankrupted by a criminal conspiracy of the food cartel in collusion with the U.S. Justice Department, also disclosed the disturbing fact that these corporate powerhouses control almost all the beef and meat processing plants and operations in the United States. In his revealing book, Stanko explains:

> The three largest choice beef processors in the United States are: Iowa Beef Packers (IBP), Missouri Beef Packers (EXCELL), and Monfort. Cargill, the international grain cartel, owns the meat giant, Excell Corporation. Armand Hammer, the Marxist oilman who is one of the premier trade arrangers for the Soviet Union, has just recently bought the huge Iowa Beef Processing Co. These processors now dominate the Midwest procurement of fed cattle and the nationwide sale of boxed beef. A twenty-five year Cargill man was made top Under Secretary of Agriculture in 1983. His name is Daniel Amstutz. He is from one of the six families of the oligopoly that control the grain companies.

> The additional five who belong to the world grain cartel which controls the transnational movements of grain and other commodities are: Con-Agra, Dreyfus, Continental, Bunge, and Andre. These companies now also dominate most domestic meat markets. Cargil controls all poultry production within Argentina. *Parade* magazine (April 16, 1972, p. 2) identified Michael Fribourg, whose family is the sole owner of Continental Grain Company and worth billions.

> Continental recently purchased and consolidated the third largest boneless beef operation in the United States, Peck Packing, from Milwaukee, while Con-Agra purchased the stock from the owners of the second largest company, Northern States. Packerland then purchased Stanko's troubled Nebraska Beef, which made them the largest

boneless beef company. These three companies are now the largest boneless beef companies on the North American Continent.[1]

The cartel allows little competition. The troubles that befell Rudy "Butch" Stanko are instructive. Stanko's fast growth and well-managed Cattle King Beef Company provided stiff competition for the global cartel. But, he and his company soon became victims. In 1982, the cartel forced a large bank to call in their loan to Stanko's Cattle King Beef Company. Rudy Stanko was able to immediately get financing from another bank unconnected to the cartel, Colorado's American Ag. However, this independent bank paid dearly for not siding with the cartel mafia. Its charter for making loans was revoked in 1984.

Ranchers Against the Wall

In the years since, things have gotten progressively worse. So much so that, in 1998, *The Wall Street Journal*, in a feature story, concluded that the consolidation of the meat industry and other problems besetting ranchers had resulted in slamming ranchers up against the wall—and putting many out of business:

> Long romanticized as symbols of self-reliance, ranchers have lately painted themselves as endangered species... Clearly, ranching's future will be dramatically different from its storied past... The number of cattle operations shrank by a quarter between 1980 and 1995. At the same time, profit margins have shriveled and conglomerates have tightened their control of the meat-packing industry.[2]

The Power of the Cartel

We see, then, that a small clique of transnational elitists

have their greedy hands on the means of food production. They can precipitate shortages to drive up prices or artificially free up massive quantities of stored grain and frozen meat to depress market prices. They give the word, and peoples everywhere are either well fed or they are deprived of sufficient food.

Even the means of distribution—how the foodstuffs are stored and transported to the local marketplaces—are in the firm grip of the cartel. In 1995, in the *New Federalist* newspaper, Marcia M. Baker reported:

> The logistical problems in handling, storing and moving
> this fall's U.S. Grain harvest—not at all a bumper crop—
> illustrate the cumulative impact of the decline in the U.S.
> transport infrastructure. And they illustrate the associated
> concentration of control of food supply lines in the hands
> of a small number of trade, shipping and processing
> companies interlocked with international financial and
> commodities interests.[3]

Baker also reported that the global cartel controlling our food supply can, when it chooses, free up resources, giving buyers "the false local appearance of there being a glut."[4] Conversely, the cartel has the unconscionable ability to stall shipments and delay transportation of grains, thus inventing food shortages.

Nothing moves unless the cartel's managers say so:

> The cartel grain merchant companies control barge lines
> and rail cars as well as grain elevators...at one Northern
> Iowa location, a train of 80 cars of grain was sitting,
> loaded, for 11 days and still not moving....Several Iowa
> elevators (not able to arrange transportation) were
> preparing to pile corn on the ground...

> "It's a mess" reported one local elevator operator. He
> stressed that the problem is not a big harvest or weather
> calamity. "The problem is logistics."[5]

The grain cartel companies—Cargill, Archer Daniels Midland, Louis Dreyfus, Continental, Bunge, and others— directly own the rail cars. "The railroad system itself is broken down." Cartel interests have also steadily bought up the nation's formerly independent grain elevators and shut them down. Thus, in a recent food crisis:

Farmers were forced into hauling grain farther and to few storage points. At the same time, the cartel grain companies moved to consolidate control of railcars, barges, elevators and all related logistics.[6]

The majority of Americans have no earthly idea that regardless of how bountiful a harvest farmers may have, a famine may, at any moment, be artificially created by a small clique of powerful global conglomerates working in tandem. All that's necessary is for the cartel to give the order and the food distribution system grinds to a crunching halt. As T.R. Reid concludes in *Feeding the Planet*, the chief threat facing humanity is not necessarily overpopulation, drought, or crop vermin and disease, but rather how food is distributed.[7]

A parallel example can be found in the oil industry. In 1973 in the United States, lines of automobiles a mile long snaked for blocks waiting for their turn at the gas pump. Yet, just offshore, off the Eastern seaboard, huge tankers filled to the brim with oil sat idly, and gasoline refineries were operating at a fraction of their production capacity. The "crisis" had been contrived from start to finish despite a much ballyhooed "oil shortage crisis."

Farmers as Slaves

Farmers have now become virtually the slaves of the cartel. The cartel jacks up prices charged the farmer to transport his crop. Then, the cartel pays whatever meager sum it chooses for the product—and the farmer just gulps and goes on, either adjusting his living standard downward and continuing to farm for only a miserable pittance of what he honestly should receive, or else abandoning family farming altogether.

If the typical harried rancher or farmer finds he cannot pay his bills—that it costs him more to produce his stock of cattle or crops than he can get on the market—he is in jeopardy of having the bank or the government credit authority foreclose on his property. Then, at auction, his home, land, buildings, and equipment are quickly bought up by the "big boys" at cut-rate prices and added to their existing vast holdings. The huge agricultural combines get larger and more prosperous, while the hard working family farmer or rancher is demolished.

Meanwhile, the consumer is hit with an inflated, ever increasing big bill for groceries at the supermarket, and he or she can't understand why. Often, the hapless farmer or rancher is blamed for the high price of food.

America at Risk

The fact that a global cartel has its vulture-like claws fastened on our food supply lines is a clear recipe for disaster. Americans who erroneously believe that the men who control this cartel have America's best interests in mind had better think again. For the elite who run the cartel, money and absolute power are the bottom line. Food can, and often is, used by the cartel as a weapon. Entire nations have been brought to their knees by cartel interests. Nations like Somalia, Ethiopia, North Korea, Haiti, and Cuba come quickly to mind. But the United States, said to be the world's only remaining superpower, is not immune. As Don McAlvany warns in his insight-filled *The McAlvany Intelligence Adviser* newsletter:

> Famine, hunger and food shortages are a way of life in much of the world. While 99-plus percent of the American populace would equate food shortages with primitive Third World nations, the very nature of modern American society has made disruptions in the food supply a distinct and growing possibility.

As in other industries, food production has become centralized, and a handful of multinational corporations wield considerable clout over the market. These firms' first loyalty is not to America, and they would be more than willing to help put the squeeze on the citizenry if it meant higher profits and a major advance towards the New World Order.[8]

Political Clout

The economic power of this global cartel translates into considerable political clout. This enables the elite to retain their monopoly control. Whichever political party is in power, the cartel pulls the puppet strings due to its financial ability to spread fortunes far and wide. In the 1996 presidential race, the cartel collectively heaped gigantic sums on the heads—and in the pockets—of incumbent President Bill Clinton and the Democratic Party. Clinton, in turn, rewarded the cartel with favorable free trade and tax legislation, environmental regulations (that discriminate against small land owners, farmers, and ranchers), and other commercial "goodies".

The Republicans, who controlled the Congress, fared equally well. One of the cartel members, Archer Daniels Midland (ADM), was so generous with its cash that Republican Party presidential nominee, Senator Robert Dole, began to be called "Senator Ethanol" (ADM is the world's largest producer of ethanol, a fuel source derived from grains). As Senate Majority Leader, Dole had worked hard to protect sugar and other price commodities with supports and subsidies (government welfare for the super-rich cartel).

America a Socialist Country?

When questioned about ADM's reprehensible use of financial "contributions" to influence politicians and recruit the government bureaucracy on its behalf, ADM Chairman Dwayne

Andreas made this startling admission: "People who are not in the Midwest do not understand this is a *Socialist country*."[9]

In other words, Andreas admitted that the top people in the agri-business and food supply industries, especially the cartel membership—knew something that the majority of Americans do not know—that there is little or no free enterprise or open market capitalism in the food and grains markets. There is, instead, government and cartel collusion. Money and government have joined hands to pad their own pockets and enhance their joint power. As Mr. Andreas frankly noted, this is the very essence of a *Socialist* form of government. In fact, the American system is little different than Fascist and Communist models, each of which, in practice, operates with a centralized government guaranteeing oligarchic control for private benefit.

However, outspokenness and candor are not character traits greatly appreciated by the cartel and its Illuminati chieftains. Following his shocking admission, Dwayne Andreas' corporation, ADM, was swiftly targeted for criminal sanctions by the Justice Department, a covert arm of the cartel's inner circle of leadership. In October, 1995, the Justice Department and FBI announced they were looking into whether ADM had violated antitrust laws by fixing prices on key agricultural commodities. Meanwhile, the Securities and Exchange Commission, the federal agency that oversees the stock and financial markets, launched an investigation into whether ADM had violated securities laws.[10]

The cartel obviously was upset over Andreas' overly revealing public remarks, and he and his corporation were now going to pay the piper. Even at that, the sentiment of insiders was that, at most, Andreas and ADM's executives and board members would be given the equivalent of a slap on the wrist—possibly sizeable fines and/or suspended sentences. Still, they were to be made an example of so that others would keep their mouths shut about the Socialist aims and organization of the cartel.

We see, then, that the cartel leadership has the power to punish its own members who err and stray from the party line or who otherwise misbehave. In the view of the elite, it is a cardinal sin to reveal facts and truths the cartel prefers remain hidden from view. The cartel's enforcement powers extend to its influence over America's trade policy through its insiders at the Commerce and State Departments. Meanwhile, the Justice Department and FBI provide for the cartel's use the law enforcement branch of government.

A License to Buy and Sell

The global cartel also carefully uses its political lobbying influence to promote its agricultural objectives within each of the 50 states. For example, in 1996, lobbyists associated with the cartel caused the state legislature of Indiana to introduce a draconian statute restricting who can buy and store grain. The proposed law included provisions to regulate fertilizer storage. According to James Henry, writer for *Agrinews Publications:*

> Anyone who buys at least 50,000 bushels of grain from a producer would have to be licensed under a bill recently passed by the House Committee on Agriculture and Rural Development.... Under the bill, the role of the Indiana Commodity Warehousing Agency would be expanded to include grain buying. Now the Agency regulates only grain storage. If the bill is approved, the agency would have the authority to examine grain buyers' records and determine whether the buyers are financially solvent. Grain buyers also would have to take a test for certification. In addition, the bill gives the state chemist the authority to regulate fertilizer storage.[11]

Who would have ever thought that in the United States of America, a license would have to be obtained from a government agency for a person or company to purchase grain? Note, also, that the Indiana bill would give the state the authority "to regulate ferilizer storage."

Increasingly, the people's freedom to buy and sell food is to be restricted and controlled. This will lead to the startling fulfillment of the Bible prophecy recorded in Revelation 13:17: "...and that no man might buy or sell save he that had the mark, or the name of the beast, or the number of his name."

Unobstructed Power

What role will the food cartel play in the coming days of hunger and chaos? To answer this question, we must understand that these powerbrokers wield unobstructed power. *They can cause food shortages even when there is an abundance of food available in the world.* The problem facing mankind today is not that farmers are not producing enough food. They are. The crisis comes about because a small band of ruthless men—the financial magnates who run the cartel—has the unfettered authority to:

1.   Set prices for commodities.

2.   Determine who can buy and sell grain and other foodstuffs.

3.   Order the transport of food supplies to proceed with

haste, or, conversely, direct a silent embargo of all means of conveyance to the marketplace.

4. Cause federal and state regulators to harass, bully, and threaten small farmers, ranchers, and others who oppose their monopoly powers.

5. Cut off fertilizer shipments to farmers, limiting the production of fertile crops.

6. Control the buying and use of seeds.

7. Reward compliant farmers with government or bank agricultural loans and punish those who refuse to "play the game" or who attempt to operate independently of the cartel.

8. Manipulate government statistics so that the consumer never really knows whether grains, corn, meat, produce and other agricultural products are in short supply, at famine levels, or in surplus.

9. With the covert assistance of military and intelligence agencies, employ satellites overhead to monitor farm production throughout planet Earth. Also, weather modification technologies can be employed to cause excessive rains and floods or droughts.

10. Direct that food supplies produced in America be sent overseas. In recent years, massive amounts of grain and other foodstuffs have been exported from the U.S.A. to Russia, China, and North Korea, causing prices to soar in America's supermarkets and food stores.

Markets are Manipulated, Americans Pay Bill

When foreign nations cannot pay for the food they receive,

the United States government funds the whole operation with billions of dollars given by the White House and the U.S. Congress through the International Monetary Fund (IMF). In other words, U.S. citizens are forced to pay more domestically for food while also being ripped by higher taxes to fund the IMF. The Illuminati's cartel prospers by selling food at market prices to bankrupt countries overseas while the American populace foots the bill.

By manipulating food supplies either to the shortage or the surplus sides of the equation, the cartel elite make money by advance buying or selling of commodities futures. It is, therefore, to their advantage to cause extreme, almost preposterous, swings back and forth in market values. Thus, in 1995 and 1996, headlines in the farm belt screamed:

"Wheat Shortages Looming"[12]

"Low Wheat Harvest Expected—50 Year Low"[13]

"Loaf of Bread to Cost More"[14]

"Agriculture Crisis Grows in Cattle and Cotton Areas"[15]

"Drought Could Mean Disaster for Grain Elevators"[16]

"World Food Shortage Grows as Surplus Stocks Dwindle"[17]

That was 1995 and 1996. However, less than 18 months later, the cartel deployed its boomerang and, presto!, suddenly the situation was reversed. Earlier, it had seemed that farmers couldn't grow enough food to fill the world's burgeoning needs. But in 1997, the world markets for grains and foodstuff began to dry up like an old piece of cracked and grayed cedar wood left out too long in the hot Texas sun. The Illuminati's currency manipulators had destroyed the economies of Asia, and the ripple effect was felt around the globe. Japan, Indonesia, Thailand, Malaysia, and other nations in Asia fell into severe and debilitating economic depression. The masses still needed food, but were too poor and too broke to pay for it.

Prices for commodities tumbled to record levels. Reporting in *The New York Times* newspaper in late 1998, Jonathan Fuerbringer reported:

> While global stock markets plunged, a major index of commodity prices on everything from oil to cotton fell to its lowest level in 21 years Thursday. Already commodity prices have fallen 20 percent in the last year and heightened the concerns about the developing world that began with the Asian financial crisis in July, 1997.[18]

Wheat shortages looming

Dwindling supplies, warning of global crisis driving up prices for grain and bread

BY BRENT JANG
Alberta Bureau

CALGARY — World wheat supplies are dipping to historic lows and warnings of global grain shortages are driving up prices and setting the stage for strong demand for Canadian wheat exports.

The developments have surprised commodity analysts, worried buyers and pleased Prairie farmers who grow much more wheat than the Canadian market can consume. About 60 per cent of Canadian wheat production is exported annually.

"There's a chance of shortages worldwide, so the prices are certain to be good," says Donna Macklin, 42, who helps run her family's farm near Grande Prairie, Alta. "We've always grown wheat."

Spot prices for some types of wheat on world futures markets have shot up 15 to 30 per cent in the past five weeks to about $240 a tonne. Wheat prices across the board have been rising gradually since February.

A drought last year in Australia and poor weather in the United States this year, combined with increased demand from China and Russia, have reduced global stockpiles of wheat.

"Supplies are expected to be as tight as we've seen since the mid-seventies," says Deborah Harri, a Canadian Wheat Board spokeswoman based in Winnipeg.

The wheat board is widely expected to increase its forecast for its benchmark wheat price, No. 1 Canada Western Red Spring, pegged now at a conservative $198 a tonne for the 1995-96 crop year. Prices also are being driven up by diminishing export subsidies in Europe and the United States.

As a result, Canadian bakeries — faced with higher bills from flour mills for the first time in three years — are expected to raise consumer prices by 5 to 10 cents for a loaf of bread.

"It's a shock to the system," says Gordon Love, vice-president of purchasing for Toronto-based Weston Bakeries Ltd. "This thing has moved so quickly, so fast. Canada may not have enough wheat to satisfy all the export customers. It's kind of scary that if there's any crop problem, we actually may have a shortage."

Canada's wheat industry touches a cross section of the economy, from family farms, bakeries and pasta makers to grain elevators, railways and shippers. The value of grain production alone this year should surpass $4-billion in Canada as the country lives up to its reputation as one of the world's main bread baskets.

Although more spring wheat was planted in Canada this year compared with 1994, yields are forecast to be lower because of weather conditions. The trend, however, has been set for wheat to make a solid comeback as undisputed "king" of crops in Canada, farm experts say.

Please see *Wheat / B10*

Although more spring wheat was planted in Canada this year compared with 1994, yields are forecast to be lower because of weather conditions.

The global cartel possesses the power to invent stupendous global food crises, even when crops are plentiful and grains, meat, and other food supplies are in abundance. The cartel can also collude either to raise the price of food commodities sky high or to depress market prices. Lower prices often decimate the livelihoods of small farmers and ranchers and favor huge, agribusiness enterprises.

Meanwhile, the *Associated Press* reported a dramatic drop in farm income:

> A worldwide grain glut and the Asian economic crisis have sent grain prices plunging. In the United States, farm income is expected to be down by fifteen percent.[19]

Farmers Take a Hit

Notice, please, that the world quickly went from a severe food shortage to a terrible glut seemingly almost overnight. Farmers (but not the cartel!) took a gigantic hit as farm income fell dramatically—"down by fifteen percent." In fact, as I discussed in an earlier chapter in this book, independent farmers in 1998 and beginning the year in 1999, suddenly found that because of the glut, it is costing them more to produce crops and to raise beef cattle and other farm animals than they are getting in income when they take their products to the market. *Consequently, farmers are plowing their wheat and other crops under and liquidating herds of cattle.*

The counter result of this destruction of excess food supplies is that as we move into the new millennium, a severe shortfall will be evidenced. Food will be in short supply. No more glut. We could, in fact, be at the beginning stages of the prophesied time of intense, worldwide hunger and famine to plague all mankind.

Strangely, even as farmers in America were plowing their excess crops under and taking damaging financial losses, reports were beginning to come in revealing that, overseas, more and more people in Asia and other Third World countries are starving and hungry. Here are just two recent news items from the *Associated Press* reflecting the growing hunger crisis:

> **India Onion Crisis Peels Away Trust.** The worst onion shortage in decades is provoking street protests, rioting, newspaper editorials, and speeches across India as angry

citizens scramble for one of the nation's staple foods...
Each person is allowed only a bit more than two pounds
of onions a week, and elaborate records are maintained to
make sure buyers don't receive more than their ration.
Earlier in the week, onion-hungry mobs looted a
government warehouse and a truck loaded with the bulb.[20]

Another Grim Year for North Korea. The harvest in
famine-stricken North Korea will be no better this year
than last year and could be worse, a senior U.N. official
said Saturday. North Korea needs about 5 million tons of
grain to feed its 23 million people but managed last year
to harvest just 2.8 million tons, said Namamga Ngongi,
Deputy Head of the United Nations World Food Program...
U.S. Officials who toured some of the hardest hit regions
of North Korea this summer said 2 million people may
have died because of famine.[21]

Weather Wreaks Havoc

In the U.S.A., massive rains were causing record floods in
Texas which covered up to one-fourth of the expansive Lone
Star State, ruining crops and destroying farms. Amazingly,
at the time the rains hit in late 1998, this area had been
experiencing one of the worst droughts on record!
Simultaneously, it was oddly reported that the severe drought
was continuing to wreak havoc in the Northern states and
threatening to turn what was one of the planet's greatest
farming regions into an arid, dry, barren dust bowl:

> Farmers in the northern U.S. say that they are facing a
> drought as serious as that of the thirties. Only the largest
> conglomerates have the chance of surviving. It appears that
> a whole generation is being turned away from farming
> which some believe will leave what once was the most
> fertile area on the earth a wasteland.[22]

This new pattern of calamitous and unpredictable weather has put many small and family farmers across the United States in a dangerous, virtually bankrupt status. Are the floods alternating with droughts simply uncontrolled acts of nature... *or* were these weather disasters conceived and executed according to a calculated, predetermined plan? Is it absurd to suggest that the government is tampering with and manipulating the weather? Could it be that there is a malevolent intent to drive farmers into despair and bankruptcy, forcing them and their families off their farms and into the cities?

Before you too hastily decide that this notion of a plot against the small farmer is too farfetched and inconceivable, may I suggest you continue reading this book. Later, as we continue our in-depth investigation of the plagues and disasters being experienced by independent farmers and ranchers, we will examine the unheralded potential for mischief resulting from the meteorological and other high tech weapons of war developed and already in the arsenals of the world's armed forces and intelligence services.

"I'm proud to be a farmer, and I genuinely enjoy most of my 60-hour weeks. But I am still not willing to do this work for free."

—Blake Hurst
Tarkio, Missouri

❧ 7 ❧

The New Colonialism—
Small Farmers Are Crushed

The strangulation and death of the small, family owned farm has long been a prime objective of the super-rich who covertly run the planet. I am convinced that this diabolical war against independently owned farms and ranches will culminate in a hunger and famine greater than any experienced in America since this nation's founding in the late 18th century.

In the pages of my groundbreaking book, *Millennium: Peace, Promises, and the Day They Take Our Money Away*, I asked the probing question, "Will starvation plague America and the globe?" My commentary in answer to that question remains just as valid today as it did back then:

During the late 70s and early 80s, there was a lot of ruckus about the plight of the farmers. You may recall that country singer Willie Nelson held a number of Farm Aid concerts attempting to raise money to keep the family farmer from going belly-up. Today, no one talks much about the farmers. What did happen to the family farmer, the guy who had only a few dozen acres? Why is the media silent?

The sad news is that most of the small farmers have left the farm and their families are now living in poverty. Cost of production forced most out of business. Farmers were forced to borrow huge sums of capital to operate and they built up insurmountable interest payments to the megabanks. Many North American farmers have gone bankrupt in the last 15 years.

The shocking facts are that these farmers' land holdings were taken over by the government and the megabanks and sold off to what can be called the super-farmers, the agribusinessmen...These wealthy agriculture combines produce the vast majority of food today. Most are owned by rich men who do not personally work the land.

This corporate takeover of American farms by the rich means that agriculture is now in the hands of just a few. The production and distribution of food has gradually been placed in the hands of the same men who control our money supply. This is frightening. It means that artificial shortages can be created instantly. There is an OPEC-type cartel operating in agriculture today....

Even the desperately poor Third World nations such as Ethiopia, Chad, Vietnam, and Peru are feeling the brunt of the food crisis. News reports indicate that world food aid shipments are at their lowest volume since 1975-76, despite millions more people in dire straits.

These desperate, hungry people include those who live in one of the world's strongest military nations, the Soviet Union. Mikhail Gorbachev, their president, has been forced to go to the United States and other Western nations begging for massive new shipments of food to keep his bankrupt Communist government solvent.

Could it be that the leader of an impoverished Soviet Union, with an angry and hungry population on his hands, will someday decide to change his nation's economic fortunes for the better by attacking in the Middle East and capturing the oil rich lands of the Arab states? This momentous event will no doubt occur. Why must it happen? Necessity is one reason. Bible prophecy, however, is the major reason this invasion of the Middle East by the Russian Bear is going to happen.[1]

As we race toward the void of the 21st century, my words in *Millennium* are taking on a prophetic cast. The consolidation of farming operations has escalated, and many thousands more farmers and ranchers have gone out of business. Meanwhile, the global cartel has tightened its grip on the production and distribution of food supplies.

In Third World countries, the economies are now in tatters. Indeed, the economic and financial crunch is also seriously impacting the richer, more technologically sophisticated nations—like France, Japan, Taiwan, Hong Kong, Singapore, Australia, and yes, the United States of America.

In earlier periods of American history, the majority of the populace were able to live off the land and eat at a subsistence level even when the stock market and other financial and industrial indicators moved southward. In more recent decades, a process of urbanization has proceeded at a rapid scale, with more and more people leaving the countryside and abandoning their farms and ranches. Increasingly, bankrupt and hurting farmers are taking up residence in the crowded cities where, devoid of advanced skills, they must work for starvation wages.

The Age of Agribusiness

Before, when the national economy dipped, country people survived through intensive labor type farming on small plots. Those days are gone. This is the age of agribusiness—of the conglomerate "farmer." There are almost no family-owned dairies, a declining number of family-owned ranches, and few family-owned farms. When the next Great Depression comes, most people will starve. People can't eat technology and computers, and they can't eat big screen TVs. Soon, when the crunch comes and the food stores lock their doors, the average American will go crazy with frustration. His family will simply go hungry.

The plight of the small farmer today will prove to be the plight of the average U.S.A. citizen tomorrow. The ongoing consolidation and centralization of food production and distribution will end in a nightmarish debacle for a hungry majority of Americans. It is, therefore, vital that we take an in-depth look at what is happening to America's farmers.

Two facts that cannot be denied are that: (1) farms are getting bigger, and (2) the number of farms is shrinking every day.

Laura Meckler writing for the *Associated Press* from Washington D.C., reported that, "The size of the American farm is increasing as the family farm of yesteryear passes from the landscape."[2]

In the same, revealing article, Meckler described the far-ranging dimensions of this dramatic change in America's farm culture:

> The Census Bureau reports that the number of farms with sales of $100,000 or more increased from 51,995 in 1969 to 333,865 in 1998. At the same time, the number of farms dropped from 2.7 million to 1.9 million, according to the report issued Monday. "It's a disturbing trend", said Bill Christison, whose farm outside Chillicothe, Missouri, has about $300,000 in sales. "Farms can no longer survive if they are too small."

"It's just totally impossible for those farmers without some economy of scale to compete", said Christison, vice president of the National Family Farm Coalition. "It's a sort of sign of the times."[3]

Lois Britt, spokeswoman for Murphy Farms of Rose Hill, North Carolina, says that the bottom line for farming is that bigger is better. "Agriculture is like any other enterprise," she adds, "The need is for tight delivery schedules, quality control, and high volume production."[4]

Murphy Farms is an operation with sales in the hundreds of millions of dollars. This huge operation relies on hundreds of smaller farmers who grow hogs on contract. In other words, many small farmers are, today, totally dependent on giant, multimillion dollar corporate farms.[5]

According to the U.S. Census Bureau, in 1992 the large corporate farms, often averaging tens of thousands of acres, produced 83 percent of farm products.[6] In 1999, it is estimated that their share has increased to 90 percent.

The big operators further accounted for 98 percent of commercial poultry production, 93 percent of vegetables and melons, 92 percent of cotton, and 91 percent of nursery and greenhouse products.[7]

Sad is the statistic that the majority of farms produced a market value of less than $100,000 and a net profit averaging less than $15,000. Small, mom and pop, family farming operations are steadily being crushed by the big boys.

Government Favors Agribusiness Combines

The policies of the United States government consistently favor the large farming conglomerates. In 1998, Congress passed legislation that the representatives and senators optimistically called the "Freedom to Farm Act." As he signed the bill into law, President Clinton bragged on all that the government is doing for the farmer. But on *Radio Free America*, a shortwave radio program, Charles Walters,

publisher of *Acres USA*, explained how the so-called Freedom
to Farm Act had "virtually destroyed the last vestige of family
farming in America."

"Factory farming," said Walters, "is now the norm, and
the future doesn't look good for small farmers."[8]

What is happening in the farm belt is ominous for
America's future, reports *Spotlight* newspaper. The elite, the
newspaper says, are transforming the entire world into a
Global Plantation. In fact, the super-rich men who have long
controlled our money supply and our banking system are
now the *New Colonialists* in charge of our food supplies.
They are the land barons and black nobility of a feudalist,
new, medieval age. Their conquest of the land is accompanied
by plutocratic "Free Trade" policies and United Nations treaties
and agreements which seemingly always work against the
economic interests of the hurting, small farmer while enriching
the super-rich agribusiness combines.[9]

The populist newspaper went on to report: "Today, farming
is big business. It's the multinational corporations that make
the profit off trade policy, not family farmers."[10]

Deceitfully, to keep the spigot of U.S. tax aid dollars
wide open and the federal largesse freely flowing into their
bulging bank accounts, the corporate chieftains who operate
these agribusiness combines hold up to the American people
the romantic notion of family farmers as the backbone of
Thomas Jefferson's vaunted agrarian society. For example,
an ad sponsored by the The Business Roundtable, a powerful,
multinational corporate lobby and planning group, shows a
solitary, hard working farmer on his tractor at dusk with the
headline, *"Don't Let the Sun Set on America's Farmers."*[11]

After capturing the sympathy of the American public
through this cunning ploy, the multinationals then go in for
the propaganda kill. They ask readers to demand that Congress
give the bankers of the elitist-run International Monetary
Fund additional billions of taxpayers' money. Help the IMF,
they explain, and you'll be helping the lonely, poor, depressed
American farmer. In fact, the IMF has never given one
greenback dollar to an American farmer—ever!

The same tactic is used over and over to convince the public that American billions for the U.N. are in America's interest, and that passage of legislation setting up a dictatorial World Trade Organization, or NAFTA, or a Multilateral Investment Treaty will help the suffering, impoverished farmer.

In reality, these Socialist programs and internationalist organizations are driving the nails into the coffin of the small family farmers while providing billions of income and extending draconian control authority to the super-rich New Colonialists who oversee the Global Plantation.

In a recent article, the respected publication, *Congressional Quarterly,* addressed the issue of the huge and profitable agribusiness industry, and demonstrated how monied interests have brought about a life and death crisis affecting the family farm:

> The agribusiness industry really controls most farmland and farmers, but the image remains of the single family farm, and that helps them enormously, said Larry J. Sabato, a University of Virginia government professor.
>
> The greater reverence in which farmers are held than, say, automakers or hardware dealers, has to do with hunger—everybody eats—and to the enduring influence of Thomas Jefferson.
>
> More than two hundred years ago Jefferson wrote, "Those who labor in the earth are the chosen people of God, if He ever had a chosen people, whose breasts He has made His peculiar deposit for substantial and genuine virtue."
>
> Even today, a beef lobbyist speaks of a "Jeffersonian agrarian ideal," and Rep. Bob Smith, the Oregon Republican, talks in almost mystical terms about how farmers convert seeds "into something that makes life sustainable."
>
> "Basically, American agriculture is being conducted in a

corporate fashion that has nothing to do with Jeffersonian agrarianism", said Merrill Peterson, a retired University of Virginia historian and biographer of Jefferson. "It was evident back in the 1930s, and before that even, that it had become strictly a mythology."[12]

Lament of Small Farmers

Blake Hurst, who works 2,800 acres with his brothers on the family farm in Tarkio, Missouri, reflecting the general mood of today's bread and butter farmer, says, "I'm proud to be a farmer, and I genuinely enjoy most of my 60-hour weeks. But I am still not willing to do this work for free."[13]

Hurst, writing in the Heritage Foundation's *Policy Review*, explains that, thankfully, a lot of people—including a number of famous name celebrities—sincerely want to help farmers. Their hearts are in the right place. The problem is that because of ignorance of the real nature of the farmers' dilemma, nothing really is getting accomplished. Adding to the farmers' woes are the new pseudo-experts, like the environmentalists, who tell farmers that if they didn't use chemical fertilizers and if they protected and honored the endangered bugs and beetles, everything would get better. Hurst laments:

> On top of cutworms, cinch bugs, weeds, droughts, floods, and bureaucrats, we farmers seem to be afflicted with more than our fair share of experts.

> The farm press in the early 80s was full of people recommending the cultivation of shiitake mushrooms and other exotic solutions to our financial woes. Now, I'm sure there is a market for shiitake mushrooms, but they could hardly solve a problem caused by $75 billion of excess debt. Then we were blessed with pictures of Jesse Jackson in overalls, Willie Nelson singing for Farm Aid, and Jessica Lange portraying a farm wife fighting for her farm. I would buy a ticket to watch Ms. Lange read the

dictionary, but her congressional testimony about farmers' problems hardly marked a high point in the public discourse.

The 90s didn't seem to be getting any better when some of these experts joined forces with environmentalists and began trying to farm from a ballot box. Fortunately, the voters exhibited some good practical horse sense this fall when they overwhelmingly voted down California's Big Green initiative, which would have banned most commercial fertilizers and pesticides.[14]

Farmers Speak From the Heart

Knowing of my heartfelt concern for their welfare and for the future of them and their families, a number of farmers have written to me at the ministry and discussed their austere situation. Some provided detailed information about the crisis in farming in general. For example, John Levrier, a friend of the ministry from Houston, Texas, sent me a news clipping from the *Houston Chronicle* newspaper headlined, "Soured on Dairy Work—Soaring Costs Forcing Farmers to Sell Milk Herds as Profits Dry Up." Here is just a portion of what was discussed in that poignant, newspaper account of financial pressures down on the farm:

> Freeman Ethridge of Sulphur Springs hadn't turned a profit on his 135 milk cows for the past year and a half. So, in April, when the protein-rich feed delivered to his farm zoomed past $10 per 100 pounds, one-third higher than normal, he decided it was time to quit.
>
> Ethridge and his family loaded the cows into trailers and hauled them to the Sulphur Springs dairy auction to be sold to the highest bidder.
>
> With that act, Ethridge joined the growing ranks of

unemployed, former "dairy farmers" in Texas who are the victims of soaring costs for feed, hay, fertilizer and fuel.

David Fowler, a co-owner of the dairy auction, sees people like Ethridge "rambling around out there, trying to find something to do."

"Some of those unemployed find a job driving a truck while others seek day labor. Listing dairy farming as skill on a resumé won't get a job," Fowler said.

The underlying problem of record feed prices is forcing smaller Texas dairy farms out of business while the biggest and strongest survive because they have deeper pockets.

Ethridge said the situation was the worst he has seen, but he was milking cows for only 10 years. "It kept getting worse and worse, finally to the breaking point," he said.

Families are going broke that have been in the dairy business for four and five generations, said Chris Clark, assistant county agent for Hopkins County. It's not just people who jumped in during the good times, he said.[15]

Everywhere one turns, one hears the mind-absorbing horror stories of small farmers, ranchers, and dairymen in distress. Often, the pitifully low price these brave, hardworking people are offered for their crops, cattle, or milk isn't enough to even pay their bills.

Recently, some kind, Christian friends of the ministry from Oregon wrote to inform us of what is going on in their state. With their letter, they included photos as documentation:

Dear Texe,

My wife and I are sending some pictures that we took of wheat fields between Pendleton, Oregon and Helix,

Oregon. We had been working on a fence in Helix on a Friday. When we went back to Helix on Monday, many of the wheat fields had been plowed under. This is the first time that we've seen this done, ever. The fields were not harvested. We figure that about half the fields were plowed. The remaining fields were later harvested, but only the ones, as far as we could tell, that had wind-damaged crops.

The price of wheat is around $2.80 a bushel, which is the point of breaking even; it's almost not worth harvesting at that price. We think the fields that were harvested were insured, and that the farmers were harvesting damaged fields, salvaging what was left after the insurance claims. If this is true, and they are doing this all around the state of Oregon and beyond, then it would be a giant step towards "Days of Hunger, Days of Chaos."

Also, the state of Idaho has just passed a ban on all pesticides on crops. This was an EPA decision. The ban will last 8 years.

Also included with this letter is an interesting sidelight on a local business. The photos of the grain elevator show that there is not much wheat being stored. The partial harvest is nearly complete. Usually, there is wheat piled up like a mountain on the asphalt. This year, nothing is visible.

The local newspapers haven't mentioned any of this as far as we know.

From another farmer friend I got the bad news that prices for cattle are at their lowest since the 1940s. This elderly gentleman wrote to tell me:

Things are hurting quite a lot due to bigger and bigger government and lie after lie. Inflation is much more than *said—last year I sold average cattle, $500 per head. So far this year, $300. Really doesn't cover the rent.*

Too wet—last year and this year. Had some hay, but no crops. The crop here is very short. Beans 4 to 10 bushels per acre where it should be 30 to 50 per acre.

Possibly the most insight-filled letter I have received is from a Christian man who is a farmer in the state of Iowa, in the very center of the grain and farm heartland. It's impossible to read what this gentleman has to say and not be brokenhearted over what is going on:

You people in Austin, Texas have very likely heard of the corn prices in Iowa and surrounding states. There are those that are making a lot of money through it, and, of course, there are those that are also getting hurt through it.

I have heard ever since last fall there is a fuel shortage worldwide. Maybe these prices for a bushel of corn are telling us something. Then again, maybe the market is controlled. I have heard rumors that next fall at harvest time, the price of corn will be way down. Who knows? Me, myself, I do not believe our feed supply is near as plentiful as it was some years ago.

I am 68 years old and have always lived in a rural area. My home, Dumont, Iowa, is a small town of 750-800 population and I have always either been on a farm or more or less associated with the farming industry. Several years ago, I would hear the smaller operators say they could not compete with the heavily government-subsidized big operator farmer. As it turned out, the big farmer operator would use his government subsidy check to buy the farm away from the smaller operator farmer. The small farmer had no choice but to leave a decent farm in the country, rural environment and move his family to a drug and crime-infested city to find work to raise his family.

Around here, the small family size farm is pretty well out of the picture. When I was 16 years old, a 160 acre farm would make a good living for a family and, very likely, have some to spare. What we have today, well, do we call that progress, or is it something else?

The same was done to the beef industry. In the hands of the rich—not the needy. The same thing is happening to the pork industry here in Iowa, like a lot of other places. The rich are taking it away from the smaller operator.

Any more, most of the hogs go directly from the feeding facility to the packing plant. And as I understand, the two are operating hand in hand through contracts. The little guy—the needy—is out. The rich are in.

All these things mentioned—Is that God's way of doing things, or is it Satan's way of doing things? Without question I believe we know the answer, don't we? I am sure we do.

Few Alternatives

These compelling, eyewitness accounts are provocative and gripping. This really *is* happening in America. The traditional farmer is being ground into the dust. He's losing his farm and his livelihood. What are his alternatives? Well, the broke farmer can pull up stakes and take whatever puny savings he still has and move to the city, where he will probably be forced to work at minimum wage. However, if he wants to stay in farm work—if his services are even needed—the displaced farmer may be lucky enough to get on with a huge farm factory—the *corporate collective*, and be paid a depressed salary.

This is the very essence of colonialism. Monied interests controlling sprawling expanses of land and territory, and a feudal system of Lords of the Manor reigning and ruling over penniless, unpropertied peasants. It is a sign of worse things to come.

> *"I couldn't keep still any longer and I blurted out (intending to be facetious), Why don't you just take everybody's money, checking accounts, saving accounts, stocks, bonds, real estate, and all their other assets and just put everything in one big pile and redistribute it to everybody in the world?*
>
> *"Our United Nation s guide replied, 'A very good idea—it's what we are trying to do here'."*
>
> —Larry Bates
> The New Economic Disorder

⅋ 8 ⅋

"Food is Power!"—They Shall Control Food, Life, and Death

"*Food is power! We use it to change behavior. Some may call that bribery. We do not apologize.*"[1] These were the threatening, blustery words of Catherine Bertini, Executive Director of the United Nations World Food Program. The occasion was the UN's World Food Summit, conducted in November of 1996. Ms. Bertini, former U.S. Assistant Secretary of Agriculture, was a feature speaker at the globalist extravaganza, and she meant just what she said.

Bertini and her globalist associates are no different than all the other pompous, diabolical, would-be world conquerors of the past. The Egyptian Pharaohs, Genghis Khan, Atila the Hun, Julius Caesar, Kaiser Wilhelm, Joseph Stalin, and Hitler—they were all basically the same. They all wanted to be gods, to control and dominate people's lives and to render death to those they adjudged unfit to live. They all had their ideological, power-hungry hirelings and lieutenants at their sides. Bertini, like Beria, Goebbels, and other servants of dictators, is one such hireling. Today, she loyally serves the United Nations Secretary General. Tomorrow, she will gladly kiss the boots of the Antichrist who heads the New World Order.

But there is a difference. A major difference. Today's UN—and tomorrow's Antichrist—possess a mighty weapon capable of driving human beings into abject slavery and servitude that Wilhelm, Stalin, Hitler, and the others did not have: *food.*

In a world that has became, in the words of a rather notorious First Lady, a "Global Village," it is food that the people of the Village must have to survive. Now, for the first time in human history, it is possible—thanks to advanced methods of control and monitoring—to use food as a battering ram to drive opponents into submission.

Before the year 2000 A.D., only isolated locales or, at most, individual nation-states, could be besieged, starved out, and conquered. Sieges of walled cities in Biblical and medieval times, and the battles of Masada, Berlin, and Stalingrad are examples. But, never was it possible to employ a totalitarian system of food control that could severely impact, simultaneously, every man, woman, and child on Earth.

Such a world system is quickly being constructed. Uri Dowbenko, writing in *The Nationalist Times*, correctly identities this new system as *"Global Techno-Feudalism."*[2] Its scope is global. It uses high technology to enforce its dictates; and the system is based on the medieval culture of feudalism. Dowbenko notes that the emerging social system,

Global Techno-Feudalism, was prescribed for man's future
long ago. H.G. Well's book, *The Open Conspiracy*, once
described its coming as a glorious thing. But George Orwell
vividly presented to us a radically different outcome—his
book *1984* outlined a "blueprint for world tyranny."

Orwell's Vision Becoming Reality?

In Orwell's dread future, food—or rather, the scarcity of
food—was an overwhelming passion. Food's provision was
the responsibility of the Ministry of Plenty, but it seemed
that there was never a plentiful supply of food to eat and
what food was available was of extremely poor quality. Because
of the great world crisis—the never ending wars and chaos—
food was rationed in the nation of Oceania. The people were
told over and over by Big Brother and his government that
things were getting better and better, that the economy was
vastly improving, that the standards of living were dramatically
rising. Of words and propaganda, there were plenty. But of
food and other necessities—there were few.

In this stark episode from the pages of Orwell's *1984*,
we witness the masterful use of propaganda by Big Brother:

...a trumpet call floated from the telescreen just above
their heads. However, it was not the proclamation of a
military victory this time, but merely an announcement
from the Ministry of Plenty.

"Comrades!" cried an eager youthful voice. "Attention,
comrades! We have glorious news for you. We have won
the battle for production! Returns now completed of output
of all classes of consumption goods show that the standard
of living has risen by no less than twenty percent over the
past year. All over Oceania this morning there were
irrepressible spontaneous demonstrations when workers
marched out of factories and offices and paraders marched
out of factories and offices and paraded through the streets

with banners voicing their gratitude to Big Brother for the new, happy life which his wise leadership has bestowed upon us. Here are some of the completed figures. Foodstuffs—"

The phrase "our, new, happy life" recurred several times. It had been a favorite of late with the Ministry of Plenty. Parsons, his attention caught by the trumpet call, sat listening with a sort of gaping solemnity, a sort of edified boredom. He could not follow the figures, but he was aware that they were in some way a cause for satisfaction. He had lugged out a huge and filthy pipe which was already half full of charred tobacco. With the tobacco ration at a hundred grams a week it was seldom possible to fill a pipe up to the top. Winston was smoking a Victory Cigarette which he held carefully horizontal. The new ration did not start till tomorrow and he had only four cigarettes left. For the moment he had shut his ears off to the remoter noises and was listening to the stuff that streamed out of the telescreen. It appeared that there had even been demonstrations to thank big Brother for raising the chocolate ration to twenty grams a week. And only yesterday, he reflected, it had been announced that the ration was to be *reduced* to twenty grams a week. Was it possible that they could swallow that, after only twenty-four hours? Yes, they swallowed it. Parson swallowed it easily, with the stupidity of an animal. The eyeless creature at the other table swallowed it fanatically, passionately, with a furious desire to track down, denounce, and vaporize anyone who should suggest that last week the ration had been thirty grams. Syme, too—in some more complex way, involving doublethink—Syme swallowed it. Was he, then *alone* in the possession of a memory?

The fabulous statistics continued to pour out of the telescreen. As compared with last year there was more food, more clothes, more houses, more furniture, more cooking pots, more fuel, more ships, more helicopters, more books, more babies—more of everything except disease, crime, and insanity. Year by year and minute by minute, everybody and everything was whizzing rapidly upwards. As Syme had done earlier, Winston had taken up his spoon and was dabbling in the pale-colored gravy that dribbled across the table, drawing a long streak out into a pattern. He meditated resentfully on the physical texture of life. Had it always been like this? Had food always tasted like this? He looked around the canteen. A low-ceilinged, crowded room, its walls grimy from the contact of innumerable bodies; battered metal tables and chairs, placed so close together that you sat with elbows touching; bent spoons, dented trays, coarse white mugs; all surfaces greasy, grim in every crack; and a sourish, composite smell of bad gin and bad coffee and metallic stew and dirty clothes. Always in your stomach and in your skin there was a sort of protest, a feeling that you had been cheated of something that you had a right to. It was true that he had no memories of anything greatly different. In any time that he could accurately remember, there had never been quite enough to eat, one had never had socks or underclothes that were not full of holes, furniture had always been battered and rickety, rooms underheated, tube trains crowded, houses falling to pieces, bread dark colored, tea a rarity, coffee filthy-tasting, cigarettes insufficient—nothing cheap and plentiful except synthetic gin. And though, of course, it grew worse as one's body aged, was it not a sign that this was *not* the natural order of things, if one's heart sickened at the discomfort and dirt and scarcity, the interminable winters, the stickiness of one's socks, the lifts that never worked, the cold water, the gritty soap, the cigarettes that came to pieces, the food with its strange evil tastes? Why should one feel it to be intolerable unless one had some kind of ancestral memory that things had once been different?...

The announcement from the Ministry of Plenty ended on another trumpet call and gave way to tiny music. Parsons, stirred to vague enthusiasm by the bombardment of figures, took his pipe out of his mouth.

"The Ministry of Plenty's certainly done a good job this year," he said with a knowing shake of his head. "By the way, Smith old boy, I suppose you haven't got any razor blades you can let me have?" "Not one," said Winston. "I've been using the same blade for six weeks myself." "Ah, well—just thought I'd ask you, old boy." "Sorry," said Winston.[3]

In Orwell's *1984*, the country of Oceania—which seems remarkably similar to what one may envision as a future Great Britain or United States following a long and protracted economic decline—had been *restructured*. This was necessary to resolve the chaos caused by foreign wars and also, people assumed, to insure the security of the state and the safety of its people. The specter of dangerous anti-government resisters constantly was before the masses. The television screen rattled on unendingly about the plot by a crazed, potentially violent, minority to overthrow Big Brother and the government.

Since Big Brother loved the people and could feel their pain, all of society hated and despised the resisters. To root them out, government security forces constantly spied on the people, using high tech means of control. Always there were show trials on TV of revolutionaries who had been recently caught plotting against Big Brother and the government. Swift punishment was invariably meted out to these dangerous resisters with their hateful insurrectionism and old-fashioned, traditional, obsolete values.

Does all of this sound hauntingly familiar to present-day America? In recent years, we have sat idly by as the government steadily has constructed around us an all-encompassing Gestapo police state possessing unwholesome powers. These terrible powers include the ability to wiretap our phones and faxes, monitor our web sites on the net, create electronic dossiers on the citizenry in cyberspace, force registration of guns, and confiscate our cash money through unconstitutional forfeiture. This Gestapo government plunders our private property under the guise of environmentalism. It controls the minds of the masses through clever "doublespeak," and it severely punishes resisters, conveniently categorizing them as inferior, politically incorrect Cretans, sick and bigoted specimens, bothersome moralists and Bible thumpers. Increasingly, any citizen who dares to think for himself is accused and prejudged as guilty of committing hate crimes and spreading antigovernment propaganda.

Why, say the brutal propaganda organs of government, should these distasteful people—these evil anti-government types—be acknowledged as having rights? Why should they be permitted the freedom to poison peoples' minds? Better either to lock them up for their hate crimes and thought crimes—or to put them out of their misery altogether. They are, after all, nothing more than worthless and useless eaters.

Times That Try Men's Souls

For any who refuse to believe what I say here is true, I beg you: open your minds and hearts to the facts. We, as Americans, are facing perilous times. Like Charles Dickens, we can honestly and soberly describe these treacherous days as "the times that try men's souls."

Is America slated to become George Orwell's prophetic nation-state, *Oceania*? What will it take to push this once, great land into the devilish void of the Orwellian black hole, to come out on the other side as a complete, seamlessly totalitarian Big Brother police state?

I firmly believe, based on years of prayerful analysis and factual investigation, that it will take only one, huge and disastrous, people-frightening crisis for America to cascade down past the point of no return to become a Kafkaesque nation with multiple chambers of horrors. The elite have planned for us just such a crisis—a moment of critical instability, the shockwaves from which are to be felt by the American affluent and poor alike. In the hoary midst of this dreadful crisis, as chaos reigns and blood is shed on the streets, drastic solutions for a *restructuring of society* will be tendered to us by our leaders—solutions we will gladly embrace. A stunned and hungry people will howl in unison, "There is no other way out."

I predict that the citizenry will eagerly junk the last vestiges of the U.S. Constitution in return for security, safety and survival. After all, not one man in a thousand can even recite half of the Bill of Rights. Not one woman in a million even knows why the founders so peculiarly, and yet so profoundly, named the first Ten Amendments, the "Bill of Rights."

How many citizens are even dimly aware that the Constitution, in its Bill of Rights, severely limits the powers of the federal government? Besides, via the means of judicial court rulings, presidential Executive Orders, bureaucratic red tape and regulations, and lax congressional legislation, most of the power and function of the first ten Amendments died off long, long ago. Today, America is a nation sagging under a gargantuan weight of thousands of banal federal and state laws, regulations, and rules. Yet, America is without a *basic law*. Would-be tyrants are no longer restrained by either the Bible or the Constitution. Certainly, they are no longer limited by the general morality level of the people. America is like a painted ship on a painted ocean, and the cunning schemers of the Illuminati have the paint brush in their smooth and satiny hands.

America is already in the process of being reconstructed and has been so for decades.

Perestroika: The Restructuring of Society

The elite are now making ready the final, climatic stages of the restructuring of American society. This process has already taken place in the Soviet Union where Communist dictator Mikhail Gorbachev and his KGB secret police introduced *Perestroika*, a Russian word meaning "restructuring or rebuilding." Everything must change, said Gorbachev. There must be

"A New Way of Thinking,...A New Global Civilization."[4]

In a stunning exposé of the *Perestroika* restructuring fraud, Russian dissident and exile Anatoly Golitsyn wrote a book called, *The Perestroika Deception: The World's Slide Toward The Second October Revolution.* Golitsyn reveals that the plan is to restructure not only Russia and the former Soviet Republics, but also the U.S.A. and Europe—indeed, the whole world. He is convinced that in Red China, Deng's "Four Modernizations" (a Chinese euphemism for "restructuring") is cut out of the same cloth. It, too, is part of the global plan.[5]

Since President Bill Clinton is well-known to be a longtime, clandestine Communist revolutionary agent, the profound implications of Golitsyn's research hits home with clarity.[6] Golitsyn also speaks with authority because he, himself, was a high official in the Soviet KGB, the secret police, when he defected to the West.

Anatoly Golitsyn, in his KGB days, actually saw the documents relative to this grand strategy of the elite. In a memo to the CIA, he reported:

> The final period of "restructuring" in the United States and Western Europe would be accompanied not only by the physical extermination of active anti-Communists, but also by the extermination of the political, military, financial, and religious elites. Blood would be spilled and political reeducation camps would be introduced. [7]

Bob Trefz, a Christian researcher and publisher of the *Cherith Chronicles*, has studied carefully Golitsyn's conclusions regarding the restructuring of America. He poses the question, why would the Communists want to assassinate people like Bill Clinton and other Communist-oriented political, military, financial, and religious elite? The answer is that revolution requires it. Having manipulated and used the first wave of treasonous associates, the overseers of the revolutionaries always dispose of them, lest they acquire too much power on their own.[8]

To the Illuminati's inner circle of leaders, the Clintons and their ilk are disposable ignoramuses to be replaced by a new set of servants—and, so the revolutionary cycle of "kill... kill...kill...kill" goes on indefinitely. Thus, Robespierre, the cruel, chief executioner during the French Revolution, was himself eventually beheaded by the slick and sharp blade of the guillotine.

Once he had laid claim to the post of Chancellor of Germany, Hitler destroyed Roehm and the Brown Shirts who had helped him gain power. Lenin quickly did away with Kerensky and the politicians who helped him overthrow the Czar, and the Ayatollah Khomeni sentenced to death the first wave of Iranian political traitors who had elevated him to the highest seat of national power. *Strong beasts always feed on inferior beasts.*

Puppets like Bill Clinton—as well as members of the Masonic Lodge and other secret societies and globalist organizations like the Council on Foreign Relations and the Trilateral Commission—had better take heed. They are considered too dangerous to let live. After the Christians and patriots are taken away, regrettably with their active assistance, they, too, will be arrested and destroyed. Their heads will be the ones on the chopping block!

> For when they shall say, Peace and safety; then sudden destruction cometh upon them, as travail upon a woman with child; and they shall not escape. (*I Thessalonians 5:3*)

"Gigantic Plans of World Salvage"

One of the globalist occult organizations fostering a New World Order is the *Lucis Trust,* headquartered in New York. Alice Bailey, the group's late founder, admitted that she received transmissions from spirit beings, whom she called the "Masters of Wisdom." These devils instructed her of what was to come. Were Alice Bailey's "Masters of Wisdom" the same devils from Satan's dimension who are now supervising the leadership of the inner circle of the global Illuminati conspiracy?[9]

This appears to be the case. In her many books, which are popular sellers in New Age bookstores, Alice Bailey makes plain that the New Age Kingdom will come about only after a great crisis. Out of chaos will come the "restructuring" of society. Everything will change.

Bailey writes that this work has been underway since the 20s by a number of groups, all supervised by the "Masters of Wisdom," to inaugurate the New Age and the future civilization.

The founder of the *Lucis Trust* also revealed that a small core group of spiritually and politically advanced thinkers, the "New Group of World Servers," make up the human element overseeing the work. Their activities are, she reports, "definitely international in scope." Through this elite core group and its influence over the masses will come about World Government, a World Economy, and the New Civilization following a great crisis and resulting chaos. The new global order will be the result of this elite cabal's *"gigantic plans of world salvage."*[10]

In 1980, World Goodwill, an offshoot of the Lucis Trust, published its pivotal booklet, *The New International Economic Order.* This constituted a detailed road map for the restructuring, or reconstruction, of society and the world, following a great economic catastrophe and world famine, followed by chaos—rioting, bloodletting, etc. Such a future catastrophe is viewed by the conspirators as a positive event because it will enable them to sweep away the last vestiges of the old order:

> In the destruction of the old world order and the chaos of these modern times, the work of the new creation is going forward; the task of reconstruction, leading to a complete reorganization of human living and to a fresh real orientation of human thinking, is taking place.[11]

Another Illuminist organization, the Club of Rome, makes

clear that the changes due to the coming economic collapse
and food crisis had to be prepared and initiated *in advance*
as part of a "Master Plan:"

> Mankind cannot afford to wait for change to occur
> spontaneously and fortuitously.... Man must initiate
> changes.... (The) crises confronting mankind now and in
> the immediate future can be successfully met provided
> there is *genuine international cooperation* in the creation
> of a *Master Plan* for world "organic growth."[12]

These same Club of Rome officials stress that, "There is
no other viable alternative to the future survival of civilization
than a new global community under a common leadership."[13]

A Redistribution of Wealth

The United Nations, with its many socialist directorates and
subsidiary organizations, is the focal point of the global
restructuring process. It is intended that following the coming
great crisis of food shortages, famine and political and social
turmoil, the world's politicians will declare that only a
revamping and restructuring of the economic system can solve
the significant concerns facing humanity.

The United Nations will propose that political democracy
and the principle of the equality of all peoples dictates that
no one group—other than the UN elite—can be permitted to
hog most of the world's scarce resources of food and water.
This "selfish behavior" cannot be tolerated, the world's media
will boldly announce.

Now, since it is the citizens of the United States that
have had so much of the world's financial and economic
riches for so long, this, it will be explained, has created a
great inequity. The UN propaganda machine will complain
that the selfish people of America enjoy too much prosperity,
goods and food, while the poverty-stricken peoples in Asia,
Central and South America, and elsewhere in the Third World

are starving and in desperate straits. Thus, the global leaders will propose that there be a *redistribution* of wealth, and that, moreover, most of the food produced and kept in America be redirected to poor nations where there is need.

Americans are to have no more or no less than people in Taiwan, Argentina, India, Haiti, and Cuba. All men equally are components of the ecological system of Earth. Therefore, all money, all wealth, all food, all goods are to be shared equally by all the people of the planet Earth. *In other words, hunger, poverty, and misery shall be endured by everyone alike!*

It is, of course, a great fallacy to suggest that inequality, either in income or wealth, is always caused by greed and selfishness. Often, a person has more than others because he or she worked harder, or longer, or smarter, and is thus more deserving. In fact, it is usually the case that abject poverty and starvation result from either the institution of a Socialist system in a country *(example*: Russia and the Soviet Union) or the adoption by the masses of false religion *(examples*: Hinduism in India; and tribalism and nativism in Africa).

The truth is that America and the West are victims of an undeserved guilt trip. As Dr. Greg McLaughlin and Jerry Huffman pointed out in a recent edition of their *Calvary Contender*:

> When we see extreme poverty and starvation, it is often due to a Socialist government and false religion (Romanism, Hinduism, etc). Despite perhaps unprecedented generosity from the West, redistributionist liberals try to make us feel guilty by saying 20 percent of the world's population uses 80 percent of the world's resources. But, as a *Christianity Today* magazine writer said, this implies that the world's resources are things found lying around, which a certain group of people has appropriated for its own use. Whereas, resources are <u>created</u>: the truth is more nearly than 20 percent of the world's population <u>creates</u> 80 percent of the world's resources.[14]

Such arguments, however rational, do not fit in with the schemes of the Illuminati elite. Their goal is not to foster and apply reason, but to grab and possess absolute power. Absolute power is only attainable if the middle class, especially in America, is destroyed and its immense wealth expropriated. America must be reduced to a feudal vassal state and the holdings and possessions of its people redistributed. Naturally, the elite will take whatever they want for themselves and then allocate the remainder for the universal masses.

Americans will be told by the media that they must sacrifice for the universal good, so that all can become one. They will also be taught that sharing of resources is a prime value in the new Global Village, for all men have the right to others' property. This very concept was, in fact, elaborated in a recent edition of *The Emergence*, a monthly newsletter of Share International, a globalist redistribution organization headquartered in London. After predicting a world stock market crash and "a period of extreme economic hardship," editor Tony Townsend suggested that:

The stock market crash will obviously lead to changes.
These have been predicted to take the form of a
reorientation of priorities by governments around the
world. Adequate food, housing, health care and education
as universal rights will become the aim. To achieve this
for all, of course, will require a fairer distribution of the
world's resources and therefore some sacrifice on the part
of the presently richer nations.[15]

Socialism—The UN Solution

The world is to be restructured to provide a Fascist form of Socialism. Remember, Hitler and Stalin were, in a large sense, ideological twins. The term "Nazi" mean "National Socialist." The Communists, too, bragged that they were Socialists. Both Hitler and Stalin taught and believed that true Socialism would *begin* in one country (Germany or Russia); then, like an octopus it would grow to encompass the entire globe. Today, the same plan is being worked by the modern-day heirs of the same Socialist elite who gave us revolutionary Nazism and Communism.

Larry Bates, astute publisher of *Monetary and Economic Review* journal, in his book *The New Economic Disorder*, touches on this plan. He writes, "I have said, for many years that the term 'New World Order' is merely a code word for one-world socialism, with an elite ruling class to govern the rest of us under their demonic system."[16]

Bates further believes that, "The mechanism that has been set up to manage us all is a world government, an antichrist system, headquartered in the United Nations."[17] In his insightful book, Larry Bates describes a visit he and several members of his editorial staff made to the United Nations in New York City:

> When we entered the U.N. complex, we were reminded at the gate that we were leaving the territory of the United States and were now entering world soil. Our purpose was to visit and explore firsthand what these folks were up to. As we entered the gate to the United Nations, that sign stuck in my mind—that although we were still in New York City, we were now on "world soil."
>
> The statue in front of the United Nations was a rider on a horse with a bow-like object drawn (which I believe is spoken of in the book of *Revelation*). A small statue featured a pistol with its barrel twisted into a knot. On one wall near the statue of the pistol was a quotation from the prophet *Isaiah*: "And they shall beat their swords into plowshares" (*Isaiah 2:4*). It was evident to me that their intent is to beat your sword and my sword into plowshares—not theirs.
>
> As we entered the main complex of the U.N. headquarters, we could see the mediation room off to our right. Also in this area is a very prominent wall-sized, stained-glass

mural depicting all of the religions of the world coming together into one...

We then journeyed throughout the complex. While in the social and economic council chambers, our young guide, a former college professor from Germany, extolled the virtues of their grand, socialist schemes.

I couldn't keep still any longer and I blurted out (intending to be facetious), "Why don't you just take everybody's money, checking accounts, savings accounts, stocks, bonds, real estate, and all their other assets and just put everything in one big pile and redistribute it to everybody in the world?"

Our United Nations guide replied, "A very good idea—it's what we are trying to do here."[18]

Proclaiming that, "The New World Order will be founded on the rule, all for one and one for all," a *World Goodwill* bulletin summarized the Illuminati's blueprint for economic control by loftily declaring:

The New World Order will recognize that the produce of the world, the natural resources of the planet, and its riches do not belong to one nation but should be shared by all...A fair and properly organized distribution of the wheat, oil, and the mineral wealth of the world will be developed ...All this will be worked out in relation to the whole.[19]

When Bailey and other New Age, New World Order propagandists banty about such loaded and misleading terms and phrases as "shared by all" and "the whole," they are *not* referring to a system of equality and democracy as we understand that term. They well know that it is the Illuminati's intent to continue its successful manipulation of the masses for its own benefit.

Thus, if all private property and lands in nations such as the U.S.A., Great Britain, Germany, Italy, France, Canada, Australia, and elsewhere can be wrested from the hands of those who rightly have title to them and rightfully deserve the rewards thereof, and turned over to the state, in reality it will fall under the absolute control of the few, the elite (i.e., The Illuminist Brotherhood).

"The Goal is Socialism"

Colonel Edward Mandell House, the founder of the Council on Foreign Relations, was President Woodrow Wilson's top foreign policy advisor. House was one of the men who first conceived the League of Nations, the U.N.'s failed predecessor. It was also Colonel House who once exclaimed: "The goal is Socialism as dreamed of by Karl Marx." Colonel House put these words in the mouth of a fictional political character in his novel, *Phillip Dru, Administrator.* This book contained the essence of the plan for achieving a unified World Government under elitist rule.

The supposedly fictional book by Colonel House was published in 1912. A year later, in 1913, the Federal Reserve Act was passed by Congress creating private—that is elitist—control over our nation's banks. The Federal Reserve is the central bank system that's to become the model for every other country's central bank. The European community is now organizing its own central bank, much like the United States' Federal Reserve.

Eventually, the Plan is to have the World Central Bank directing and in charge of all regional and national banking centers.

Colonel House's 1912 book was also followed a year later by the 16th Amendment to the Constitution, setting up the Internal Revenue Service (IRS). Up to that time, in the U.S.A. there was no federal tax on people's personal earnings. Today, the IRS and its brutal system of extracting money from citizen victims is the pride of the New World Order's dictatorial leadership. *They are now proposing that the United Nations be given the authority to globally tax individuals and nations.*

To make this global tax proposal more palatable to the masses, especially in America and the West, the Illuminati intends to use the media to propagandize the message that the UN will help the average citizen and only tax the super-rich. One proposal is to slap a tax on each barrel of oil that is shipped from the Persian Gulf. The money collected, the story goes, will be used to clean up the world's polluted environment. Who can be against such a worthwhile objective?

This is the same, deceitful fable that American citizens were told back in 1913. Woodrow Wilson, his mentor, Colonel House, and their cohorts in Congress and the media were able to convince the American people that the federal income tax would never be levied on the average worker. It was promised that only a tiny percentage of the very rich would ever have to file, and they would pay in taxes only a small amount (less than two percent of their net income). But once the elite got what they wanted with passage of the 16th Amendment, the floodgates were opened wide. Today, it is the great middle class—the vast majority of working people— who are taking on an inordinate load. And our taxpayer dollars are used for foreign aid and to bankroll the UN, the World Bank, and the IMF. Indeed, the income tax burden has now reached an oppressive level for the average American.

President Wilson was able to advance the Illuminati plan two steps closer to fulfillment with the enactment of the Federal Reserve Act to control banks, and the 16th Amendment to the Constitution which provided for an individual and corporate income tax. But Wilson and Colonel House, both of whom abhorred and detested the American constitutional system of government with its three branches of government and its check and balances, failed in their corrupt aspiration to advance the plan a giant leap forward by having the U.S.A. join the *League of Nations.*

Finally, the Congress began to wake up and smell the roses. The Senate was able to frustrate the internationalist schemes of Wilson, House, and their internationalist conspiracy crowd by rejecting Wilson's proposal for American entry into the *League of Nations*, the predecessor to today's United Nations.

But amazingly, in 1917, only five years after Colonel House's Illuminist book, *Phillip Dru, Administrator,* which called for a world government was published, a series of bloody and strange events in the Russian empire catapulted Lenin and the Bolsheviks (Communists) to power in Moscow. The Communist vanguard then promptly put in motion their utopian plan to bring all the Earth together under *one* governing body.

We now know that Marx, whose 19th century writings later inspired the overthrow of the Czarist monarchy and the takeover of Russia by a Communist elite, was a stooge and accomplice of the world revolution conspiracy of the powerful Illuminati. And that Vladimir Lenin and his "dictatorship of the proletariat" began immediately to cooperate with the money, banking, and industrial combine of the Illuminati shortly after they seized control of the Kremlin.

Suddenly, the conspirators had their grimy hooks fastened onto an expansive empire—the U.S.S.R.—which gave them a tremendous opportunity to advance their global cause.

The Glory of the One

What must be clearly understood about the Illuminati's enduring blueprint for world domination is the subversion of the *democratic principle.* This is a principle which now has completely captured the minds and hearts of the six billion inhabitants of planet Earth; yet, the universal yearning for democracy is the primary means by which the conspirators intend to attain their objectives. The Illuminati seeks to set up a New World Order in which a multitude of powerful United Nations agencies and institutions present an *illusion* of popular control. But in fact, the whole system is manipulated behind the curtains like some hideous and sinister type of global puppet show.

If the world's peoples could only be aided to understand this evil intent by the elitists to subvert true democracy, their insidious plot might be stopped dead in its tracks. Regrettably, the world seems to be buying the fog and light show that is fostered by media propagandists. The average man and woman simply cannot fathom, nor protect themselves against, the incredible mind control technology being employed.

The general public is certainly not aware that the Illuminati use an Orwellian system of doublespeak and Illuminist coding in the messages it transmits to the world's populations. For example, in late 1991, World Goodwill, an organization headquartered in three world capitals—New York, London, and Geneva—which has vast influence in promoting the internationalist schemes of the Illuminati, sent out a bulletin announcing the celebration of a "New Group of World Servers Festival Week," to be held December 21-28.[20]

Explaining that, "At this time of planetary crisis, millions of people around the world know that meditation and prayer can be a powerful force in helping to build a more just and integrated global order," World Goodwill invited people everywhere to participate with the elite of the New Group of World Servers in the invoking of the following mantra of prayer:

May the power of one Life pour through the group of all true servers.

May the love of the one Soul characterize the lives of all who seek to aid the Great Ones.

May I fulfill my part in one Work through self-forgiveness, harmlessness, and right speech.[21]

Participants were asked to link-up and recite this prayer and mantra "with focused attention" everyday at 5 p.m. local time. World Goodwill stated that, in this way, "spiritual energy would be transmitted to strengthen world unity and right human relationships."[22]

No doubt, tens of thousands of Americans, Europeans and others did, in fact, participate in this World Goodwill event, since this organization, because of its world clout, has untold numbers of followers. However, how many who participated truly understood that the words in the mantras they were reciting were carefully designed by thought control experts to effect a *conditioning* of the mind? How many of these sincere, but misguided, people actually comprehended *who* the "Great Ones" are that they pledged to aid? How many understood completely the goals and ramifications of the *"work"* of which they were agreeing to be a part?

Certainly, participants were not aware of the colossal changes that are integral to the Illuminati's Master Plan. These changes, the end results of the planned restructuring process, include:

1. The mandatory termination of the family farmer and rancher and the collectivization of all lands and agriculture.

2. The establishment of a *World Food Authority* to oversee the global production and distribution of food and commodities.

3. The formation of a planetary, socialist government.

> "What I am promoting is the reorganization of the world."
> —President Bill Clinton

> "The Consitution of the United States needs to be reconsidered and altered...to create a whole new structure of government...The System that served us so well must, in its turn, die and be replaced."
> —Alvin and Heidi Toffler
> The New Civilization

❦ 9 ❦

The New Civilization

The coming days of hunger and chaos, with resulting global economic and social breakdown, will present a unique opportunity for the Illuminati. Now comes their planned era of *Perestroika*, or reconstruction. As Alice Bailey once trumpeted, "Out of the spoliation (spoil) of all existing culture and civilization, the New World Order must be built."[1]

Before the crash and crisis, the masses could not be easily moved to submit to the government's use of dictatorial means. However, after the fall, millions of voices will rise up to demand immediate change. A hungry and starving populace is not patient.

President Bill Clinton, a member of the Bilderbergers, the Trilateral Commission, the Council on Foreign Relations, Freemasonry, and just about every other Illuminati front group, is one who has dutifully carried out the directives passed down to him by his hidden chiefs. Upon his election, the newly inaugurated President echoed the word "change" every opportunity he got. He continually repeated the phrase, "It's the economy, Stupid," when referring to the means for winning over and persuading the masses. Clinton and his Vice President Al Gore continually speak of "reinventing government."

The Reorganization of the World

At a news conference while visiting Argentina on October 19, 1997, when asked by local reporters about his agenda for South America, President Clinton gave this mind-warping response: *"What I am promoting is the reorganization of the world."*[2]

It is, in fact, an entirely revolutionary *New Civilization*—the "reorganization of the world"—that we are expected to swallow and like. Often called the *"Third Wave,"* this New Civilization is to be a colonial paradise in which the elite will control the great bulk of private property—including farm lands and the means of production. The liberties of the people will be severely circumscribed, and the principles enumerated in America's Bill of Rights swept away and extinguished.

Perhaps the best expression of the Illuminati's intent in promoting this New Civilization is found in the book, *Creating a New Civilization,* by Alvin and Heidi Toffler. The foreword to the Tofflers' book is written by Newt Gingrich, Republican from Georgia and former Speaker of the House of Representatives. Gingrich was so smitten by this demonic book (which has a green-colored symbol that appears to be serpentine on its cover) that he once distributed a copy to all 465 members of the House of Representatives.[3]

The Tofflers are former labor union organizers. Their book is a mini-guide to the Third Wave economy, religion, and political system. Here are just a few of the shocking, Fascist-oriented proposals and declarations contained in *Creating a New Civilization*:

> A new civilization is emerging in our lives. This new civilization brings with it new family styles, changed ways...a new economy, new political conflicts, and... an altered consciousness...Humanity faces a quantum leap forward. This is the meaning of the Third Wave.[4]

> Our argument is based on what we call the "revolutionary premise"....The revolutionary premise liberates our intellect and will.[5]

> Nationalism is... First wave. The globalization of business and finance required by advancing Third Wave economies routinely punctures the national "sovereignty" the nationalists hold so dear... [6]

> As economies are transformed by the Third Wave, they are compelled to surrender part of their sovereignty...Poets and intellectuals of Third Wave states sing the virtues of a "borderless" world and "planetary consciousness."[7]

> The Constitution of the United States needs to be reconsidered and altered... to create a whole new structure of government...Building a Third Wave civilization on the wreckage of Second Wave institutions involves the design of new, more appropriate political structures...The System that served us so well must, in its turn, die and be replaced.[8]

In this looming colonial paradise on Earth, the primary method of control of the masses will be food. Napoleon once said, "An army travels on its stomach," emphasizing the significance of food to health, morale, and will. The Illuminists believe the world can be restructured and rebuilt with a system

devised so that the masses can be inspired and motivated—
or repressed and beaten down as need be—by either making
food liberally available or denying it.

This, then, is the agenda for a New Civilization based on
the "wreckage" of current civilization. With people hungry,
starving and craving for change and the restructuring of a
"New Deal," the Illuminati are confident that the masses will
go along with the altering of the Constitution of the United
States and the effective end of national sovereignty. In their
state of mental confusion and physical misery, with their
cupboards empty of food, the conditioned masses will be
ready for, in the words of the Tofflers, "a new economy...
new family styles...the globalization of business and finance...
and a borderless world and planetary consciousness."⁹

A Blueprint for Managed Foodcare

The new economy will evidently include a provision for
government management of our food supply. Indeed, a startling,
1996 article in *The Wall Street Journal* outlined a *"Blueprint
for Managed Foodcare."* Written by Karl-Otto Liebmann,
associate clinical professor at Yale University School of
Medicine, *The Wall Street Journal* piece was said by some
to simply be a wry satire or cynical argument against the
Clinton administration's proposed managed healthcare plan.
But others saw in the article by Liebmann a more sinister
agenda. They asked, could this be the beginning of a
propaganda campaign to desensitize Americans to eventually
accept an Orwelian system in which the federal government,
or a global government, minutely controls America's food
supplies and even the eating habits of its people?

Please examine below some of what Dr. Liebmann proposes
in his shocking *The Wall Street Journal* article and come to
your own conclusions:

> The time has come for the eating public to face a stark
> reality: The consumption of food, if allowed to grow at the

present rate, will bankrupt our great nation. Production of food has risen from 10% to more than 30% of the gross domestic product since 1945. The Congressional Budget Office projects that by the year 2010, Americans will spend more money and time on eating than on working, vacationing, and being sick combined.

To counter this threat, a junior U.S. Senator (whose name has been withheld upon request) has begun to draft legislation designed to fundamentally reform the way Americans consume food. The proposal, preliminarily dubbed "Managed Foodcare," promotes the cost efficient consumption of food by regulating access to stores and restaurants.

A brief outline will illustrate how the reforms benefit the average eater. Each year, during the last week of December, consumers have the choice of signing up at their preferred grocery store or restaurant for the year to come. These two main retail markets for the distribution of food are referred to as Primary Food Providers...
Consumers will be obliged to buy all their food at the chosen store and eat at the restaurant they elected. There will be a designated copayment, and together with their employer, they will also pay a monthly premium to a Food Management Organization (FMO).

FMOs, whose formation will be encouraged under the legislation, are privately owned corporations. They control the production and manage the distribution of food based on a highly variable Cost Efficiency Quotient, whose numerical value is directly proportional to the value at which the FMOs' stocks are traded on the open market. FMOs contract with Primary Food Providers to provide the most cost-efficient nutrition to their enrollees...

Basically, stores and restaurants will receive a fixed annual amount of money from their FMO for each enrolled customer, regardless of how much or little he consumes during the year. If the enrollee spends more than his allotment, it will be the provider's loss; if less, it will be the provider's gain. FMOs will maintain personal customer records listing all purchases, creating an "Individual Consumption Profile" (ICP) for each member. The ICP is subject to periodic review and approval by the FMO. People with excessive ICPs are considered "high risk" and may eventually lose their right to be reenrolled in any FMO. (Soup kitchens and self-help groups will no doubt assist these misfits.)

The proponents of Managed Foodcare sum up their argument by pointing out that their proposal preserves and protects genuine American values... Ultimately, Managed Foodcare will accelerate the accumulation of capital in the hands of those who know best how to promote a healthier and leaner America.[10]

I do not think Dr. Liebmann seriously wants this heinous program of food rationing through bureaucratic oversight to be adopted. But, there are some who do. As we shall see, a number of very serious proposals are at large. Peoples' minds are being brainwashed to accept the "sharing principle" of Socialism—that only a mandatory food redistribution program will guarantee that all people, of every economic strata, have *equal access* to food. That being so, then it follows that, because of the inequity in income between the rich and poor nations, food must be forcibly taken away from affluent countries like the U.S.A. so that Americans eat no better in caloric intake and food choice than, say, people in Mexico, Honduras, or Ethiopia.

The Murderous Nature of Collectivism

We return once again, therefore, to the "collectivism" philosophy of the Fascist-oriented Illuminati elite. They yearn

THE WALL STREET JOURNAL WEDNESDAY, JANUARY 10, 1996

Blueprint for Managed Foodcare

By KARL-OTTO LIEBMANN

The time has come for the eating public to face a stark reality: The consumption of food, if allowed to grow at the present rate, will bankrupt our great nation. Production of food has risen from 10% to more than 30% of the gross domestic product since 1945. The Congressional Budget Office projects that by the year 2010 Americans will spend more money and time on eating than on working, vacationing, and being sick combined. To counter this threat, a junior U.S. senator (whose name has been withheld upon request) has begun to draft legislation designed to fundamentally reform the way Americans consume food. The proposal, preliminarily dubbed "Managed Foodcare," promotes the cost-efficient consumption of food by regulating access to stores and restaurants. It preserves the principles of consumer choice and free competition.

A brief outline will illustrate how the reforms benefit the average eater. Each year, during the last week of December, consumers have the choice of signing up at their preferred grocery store or restaurant for the year to come. These two main retail markets for the distribution of food are referred to as Primary Food Providers. Employers will by law be required to offer employees a choice among at least three so-called Food Benefit Plans. FBPs describe what stores, restaurants, kinds of food and menus will be covered by the plan. FBPs will also furnish comprehensive brochures listing the items approved, such as certain cereals, vegetables, meats, and so on.

The lawmakers anticipate that the opportunity to choose only once a year what to eat for the next 12 months will save families innumerable hours of time now spent on gazing at store shelves or menus and comparing brands and prices. During the year of the plan, consumers will be obliged to buy all their food at the chosen store and eat at the restaurant they elected. There will be a designated copayment, and together with their employer, they will also pay a monthly premium to a Food Management Organization.

FMOs, whose formation will be encouraged under the legislation, are privately owned corporations. They control the production and manage the distribution of food based on a highly variable Cost Efficiency Quotient, whose numerical value is directly proportional to the value at which the FMOs' stocks are traded on the open market. FMOs contract with Primary Food Providers to provide the most, cost-efficient nutrition to their enrollees.

The key element of the reform is known as "capitation." Basically, stores and restaurants will receive a fixed annual amount of money from their FMO for each enrolled customer, regardless of how much or little he consumes during the year. If the enrollee spends more than his allotment, it will be the provider's loss; if less, it will be the provider's gain.

Legislators from New York and California have objected that some people habitually eat more than others or have developed rather idiosyncratic and expensive tastes. Such behavior, comparable to the reckless spending of health dollars by people with chronic or terminal illnesses, could quickly bankrupt the provider. To counter this fiscal threat, the FMOs will maintain personal customer records listing all purchases, creating an "Individual Consumption Profile" (ICP) for each member. The ICP is subject to periodic review and approval by the FMO. People with excessive ICPs are considered "high risk" and may eventually lose their right to be re-enrolled in any FMO. (Soup kitchens and self-help groups will no doubt assist these misfits.)

To rein in abuse of specialty shops and gourmet restaurants, access to these establishments will be controlled by the primary food providers. They will serve as "gatekeepers" and decide whether and when a consumer should be referred to specialty providers such as Italian bakeries or French restaurants. Their decisions will be guided by their conviction that packaged breads and cakes or fast food can meet the same nutritional needs as delicatessen foods. They also recognize that the more money from a fixed, capitated amount that consumers spend on outlandish food, the less will remain for primary food providers.

The proponents of Managed Foodcare sum up their argument by pointing out that their proposal preserves and protects genuine American values. The new laws support yearly renewable consumer choice, and at the same time reduce unnecessary and costly culinary options. They encourage corporate and individual responsibility by rewarding thoughtful management of food supply and demand. Capitation will further thriftiness, invention, and imaginative sales practices. Ultimately, Managed Foodcare will accelerate the accumulation of capital in the hands of those who know best how to promote a healthier and leaner America.

Dr. Liebmann is an associate clinical professor of psychiatry at Yale University School of Medicine.

This article in **The Wall Street Journal** *suggested that the government found a Food Management Organization (FMO) to operate a "managed foodcare" program which would limit citizens' access to food. While the author's intent may have been merely to criticize the Clinton Administration's proposed Socialist healthcare plan, in fact, many influential politicians, financiers, and other power-brokers are intent on establishing a managed foodcare program in the U.S.A.*

to sit atop a societal pyramid of peons, peasants, and serfs, whose lives are supervised and guided by technocrats and politicians who devotedly serve the Illuminati and the system. The relatively few members of the Illuminati hierarchy will sit at the apex of the pyramid. In terms of agriculture and food production, the restructuring of society will result in *collective farms,* defined in *Webster's* dictionary as: "A farm, especially in a Communist country, formed from many small holdings collected into a single unit for joint operation under governmental supervision."

History provides many poignant examples of famine resulting from forced collectivization. In the Soviet Union in the 1930s, Communist Party chieftain Joseph Stalin supervised a holocaust that had far more brutality, suffering, victims and casualties than the German holocaust of the Nazis. Drawing on the study, *Utopia in Power,* by Soviet expatriate authors Mikhail Heller and Aleksandr Nekrich, *The New American* magazine recently published a tremendously insightful article examining Stalin's atrocities in the Ukraine:

> The Ukrainian famine was produced by the Soviet govern-
> ment's drive to collectivize that nation's agricultural
> system, which for centuries had been the "granary of
> Europe."...To break the resistance of Ukrainian farmers,
> the Soviets attempted to herd them onto *kolkhozes,* or
> state-owned collective farms. Those who held out were
> denounced as "kulaks" or *podkulachniki* ("kulak
> henchmen"). "Either we go backward to capitalism or
> forward to socialism," declared Stalin. The Soviets insisted
> that repressive measures in Ukraine were made necessary by
> the insidious actions of "insurrectionists," "terrorists," and
> "wreckers."

> One of the most haunting images associated with the Nazi
> Holocaust is that of men, women, and children being
> herded into boxcars destined for the Polish extermination
> camps. Once again, Hitler merely followed the model
> created by Stalin. Kulaks and their 'henchmen' were
> deported with all of their families, including infants and
> old people... Hundreds of thousands were shipped in
> unheated boxcars thousands of kilometers away to remote
> parts of the Urals, Siberia, and Kazakhstan. Many died
> enroute; many others died after their arrival, for as a rule
> they were deported to uninhabitable locations...

> In 1937, Soviet expatriate writer Walter Krivitsky
> described the scene he came across at a railroad station in
> Kursk during the dekulakization campaign: "In the waiting

area there were nearly six hundred peasants—men, women, and children—being driven from one camp to another like cattle... Many were lying down, almost naked, on the cold floor. Others were obviously dying of typhoid fever. Hunger, torment, and despair were written on every face.

Those who remained in Ukraine fared little better. In 1932, as depicted in the Canadian documentary *Harvest of Despair*, the Soviet government dispatched an army of Chekists (secret police) and Party members to collect all of the grain from the collective farms—including the chaff—and to guard all stores of food and livestock against the starving population. Soviet military and security forces also sealed off Ukraine's borders.

The clear intention was to slaughter as many Ukrainians as possible through the protracted agony of hunger. In many tragic instances, the victims were reduced to cannibalizing those who perished.

A definitive casualty count of the terror famine has never been, and will never be, determined exactly, note Heller and Nekrich. The losses of livestock were calculated, on the other hand, down to the last sheep. The Soviet government ceased to publish birth rates and mortality figures in 1932.[11]

How many Ukranians did perish in the savage years of forced collectivization? Heller and Nekrich write:

In 1935, Soviet Foreign Minister Molotov reported that where the kulaks had numbered 5,618,000 in 1928, only some 149,000 survived collectivization. Chekist official Aleksandr Orlov estimated that the famine claimed up to seven million victims.

In 1974, Soviet demographer Boris Urlanis noted a population loss of 7.5 million between the end of 1932 and the end of 1933—the period in which the engineered famine was at its height. At about the same time, underground Soviet writer I.G. Dyadkin published an essay presenting the case for a casualty count of 15.2 million people. Stalin himself boasted—yes, boasted—to Churchill in 1943 (of) reprisals against "ten million kulaks," the vast majority of whom were slaughtered, and the rest sent to Siberia.[12]

Could a murderous program of Socialist collectivization be forced someday soon on the American people? *Absolutely!* We should harbor no doubts that this dark menace is exactly what is intended for our bleak future. Environmental collectivists have already put forth stark, monstrous proposals to return the great bulk of America's well-developed agricultural communities and the small towns and villages that service them to primitive nature—into wildlands. Environmental organizations like Earth First call this the "Rewilding of America."

Through governmental police powers, to save "Mother Earth" and insure a "sustainable environment," it is proposed that tens of millions of farmers, ranchers, small town residents, and other citizens be driven off their lands. Their homes, farms, and businesses—complete with all fences, barns, highways, and roads—are to be bulldozed and grazed over. The resulting deserted territories will be declared "off-limits for human habitation."

Under "Rewilding," food production will be reserved for only a few, gigantic agribusiness collectives owned and operated by multinational corporations favored—and in bed with—the government.

Beware America's Secretaries of Agriculture

The coming forced collectivization of America will probably be administered by a number of different government bureaucrats, working in tandem with Socialist-oriented environmental organizations. You can count on the bureaucrats at the Environmental Protection Agency, the Interior Department, the Army Corps of Engineers, the U.S. Fish and Wildlife Service, and the Department of Justice to be at the forefront in organizing the "Rewilding" collectivization program. The FBI and BATF will provide the spies and the firepower to intimidate and bully hapless farmers, ranchers, and other citizens and force them off their land. The Department of Justice will assist in prosecuting as "eco-criminals" those citizens who stubbornly refuse to leave their homes and businesses.

Then there's the U.S. Department of Agriculture (USDA). Through the first few decades of its existence, the USDA focused on service to farmers and food consumers. But under "Rewilding," the department will take on a wholly new character. In fact, for a number of years now, Secretaries of Agriculture—appointed to their office by the President—have been chosen for their posts based on their loyalty to collectivist views and their fealty and dedication to the agribusiness cartel.

In the 1930s, President Roosevelt appointed as head of the Department of Agriculture Henry Wallace. Wallace, an avowed, dyed-in-the-wool Socialist, was, like his boss, FDR, a high-ranking initiate of the Masonic Lodge. It was Wallace and FDR who conspired together to change the U.S. currency's one dollar bill to add the ominous pyramid and all-seeing eye of Osiris, the Egyptian sun god and his son, Horus, a deity revered in Freemasonry. On the dollar bill, just under the symbol of the eye and pyramid, is the Latin inscription, *Novus Ordo Seclorum.* Simply interpreted, this means "New World Order," but it is also given a broader meaning of "New World Order apart from God."

Henry Wallace, being an Illuminist, was deeply involved in satanic worship and New Age theology. He was an intense student of the Luciferianism of Guierdjeff and Nicholas Roerich. After leaving the Department of Agriculture, Wallace ran for the high office of President of the United States on the Socialist Workers Party ticket. This party's dogma and platform came almost verbatim from the Communist Party line. Keep in mind that during this same time frame, Stalin and his secret police were busy murdering millions of Ukranians and forcibly evicting farmers off their lands in a heinous program of government confiscation and terror. Wallace and Stalin were ideological partners in this collectivization nightmare.

Today, America is dominated by Masons and members of secret societies. Most presidents of the United States are Masons. Some of the most powerful congressmen and the bulk of the judiciary are ranking Masons. Members of the Masonic Lodge and other secret societies also dominated Germany in the days leading up to the Great Depression of the 1930s. Adolf Hitler, too, was a member of secret societies. Berlin became notorious for its decadent café society, its nightspots, and its drunken all-night revelers. Notice the Mason Shriner "fez" cap on this Berlin party-goer, signifying he is a Lodge brother of fellow Masons Franklin D. Roosevelt and Henry Wallace. The parallel of the Germany of the 1920s and 1930s with modern-day America may well be highly significant.

It was during this same era that President Roosevelt, Wallace, and their Agriculture department bureaucrats came up with their farm price support and crop quota programs for the United States. But if the two Masonic brothers could have gotten what they *really* wanted, the process of Communist collectivization would have achieved far greater objectives.

A New Constitution of a Restructured America

FDR and Wallace chose as Assistant Secretary of Agriculture a third Masonic associate, Rexford Tugwell. Tugwell was at the time a propagandist for international banking interests and was principal author of *The Newstates Constitution.* This document, produced with millions of dollars in grants from the Ford Foundation, was intended to replace the original Constitution given us by our founding fathers. It would have reduced Americans to the status of economic serfs and erected a dictatorship of the elite on American soil.

As Assistant Secretary of Agriculture, Rexford Tugwell lobbied incessantly with Congress and with the media for the Illuminists' infamous plot to steal and confiscate private property and lands. In 1934, a revealing article was published by a newspaper in Helena, Montana, and in a number of other newspapers regarding Tugwell's campaign to "reform American agriculture." Tugwell minced no words about the fact that the Roosevelt administration favored the unconstitutional confiscation of farms and control by the government of all privately owned land:

> Helena. (UP) — Use of all land, public and private will be controlled by the federal government in the future, Assistant Secretary of Agriculture Rexford Tugwell predicted this week.
>
> Land which cannot be operated effectively under private ownership will be held by the government as public

forests, parks, game preserves, grazing ranges, recreation centers and the like, Tugwell asserted.

Privately owned land will be controlled "to whatever extent is found necessary for maintaining continuous productivity," he said.

State officials here were studying Tugwell's statement today to see how his prediction might affect Montana.

"We have depended too long on the hope that private ownership and control would operate somehow for the benefit of society as a whole. That hope has not been realized," said Tugwell.

Tugwell said present acreage reductions plans were only an emergency stop gap. "What is done is merely to keep a part of each field of each farm out of use," he said. "It seems to me obvious that this cannot be a characteristic feature of a permanent policy."

As an alternative, Tugwell advocated controlling the total volume of farm products by limiting the area available for production, the government acquiring and devoting to other uses all land in excess of that needed for production.

He envisioned "a commercial agriculture made up of the most efficient farmers operating the best of our lands."

"Contrary to the desired trend, two million persons have returned to farms during the depression," he said.

"We already had too many farmers," Tugwell said. "We could probably raise all the farm products we need with half our present farmers, or twelve and one-half percent of our total working population."

"Private control has failed to use wisely its control of the land," he concluded. "We are preparing a land program not merely for the benefit of those who held title to it but for the greater welfare of all the citizens of the country."[13]

Of Potatoes and Survival

During the FDR-Wallace-Tugwell years, the White House and Congress passed the unbelievable Potato Control Act. This law would have assigned a quota to how many potatoes each farmer could grow and market. Any potatoes sold in excess of the quota must bear a government issued stamp and pay a tax fee on each bushel. Further, any farmer who sold unstamped potatoes, or any housewife or individual who bought such unstamped potatoes, would be subject to a fine and jail sentence.

If it had not been for a brave U.S. Supreme Court, which nullified the Potato Control Act in 1935, declaring the law a gross violation of the Constitution, this would have been the first of an avalanche of such Communist-oriented agricultural laws and regulations. In retaliation for their defiance, the judges of the court were vilified by President Roosevelt and his political allies and branded "reactionary neanderthals."

The treacherous un-American activities of Masonic President Franklin D. Roosevelt and his Agriculture Department co-criminals were amply documented in a highly documented book by Dan P. Van Gorder, *Ill Fares the Land: The Famine Planned for America.* Van Gorder's book is, regrettably, now out of print, but its analysis of the general plan to induce famine in America still holds true, except that, today, the plot of the elite is greatly advanced. In his book, Van Gorder warned that "our national survival is in serious jeopardy."[14]

"We are engaged," wrote Van Gorder, "against an enemy entrenched deeply within our governmental structure and rapidly gathering its forces without, an enemy whose plans for world conquest were completed, and announced, long ago."[15]

Van Gorder correctly suggested that, "famine is the last thing we would expect or suspect."[16] Yet, it is through hunger and famine that the conspirators hope to attain their selfish goals.

Hidden Messages of Illuminist Puppets

During the presidency of Jimmy Carter, yet another Illuminist Secretary of Agriculture was appointed: Orville Freeman. Freeman, a New Ager, is a member of both the Club of Rome and The World Future Society. In his report, *Grain and Food Cartels Wage War on America and Europe,* researcher Dr. John Coleman exposes Freeman's ties to the super-rich agricultural cartel. He says that Freeman, as Secretary of Agriculture, heavily promoted genocidal Malthusian policies of depopulation. For example, he once proposed that, "The owners of lands in Third World countries be matched with corporate giants of the advanced sector."[17]

This is interpreted by Coleman as a prime example of the hidden messages imbedded in the language of people like Freeman, who, says Coleman, was a master at Orwellian "doublespeak." What Freeman had in mind was actually the confiscation of the lands by the elite, with the full cooperation of the United Nations, the International Monetary Fund, and other globalist power groups.

Fast-forwarding up to today, we find the same kind of New World Order puppets holding sway at the Department of Agriculture in Washington, D.C. President Clinton's choice of Mike Espy as Secretary of Agriculture resulted in Espy's resignation under fire after accusations the Agriculture Secretary had taken gifts from agribusiness bigwigs. Espy's infraction was investigated by an independent prosecutor; he was indicted but was acquitted by a court jury.

Clinton's present man holding forth as Secretary of Agriculture is Dan Glickman. Glickman is simply a yes-man who continues the anti-small farmer and rancher policies of his predecessors. Like his historical teammate, Henry Wallace,

Glickman is a high-ranking Mason. The February, 1998, issue of *The Scottish Rite Journal,* the official publication of the Supreme Mother Council, Scottish Rite Freemasonry, Washington, D.C., proudly reported that "Brother Dan Glickman," Secretary of Agriculture, had been elevated to the prestigious 33rd degree of Freemasonry.[18]

The Scottish Rite Journal heaped praises on their new, 33rd degree Masonic brother, noting that Glickman is a former United States Congressman from Kansas. He was also reported to be "a member of Albert Pike Lodge No. 303, Wichita, Kansas." Glickman, the publication added, "was made a Master of the Royal Secret in the Valley of Wichita in 1986 where he was elected the Class Representative in his Scottish Rite Class." The same article said that, "Glickman holds the Active Legionnaire Honor in the Demolay."[19]

"It is good," a high ranking fellow 33rd degree Mason

Left, Secretary of Agriculture Dan Glickman, on a photo opportunity tour posing as a friend of beleagured small farmers. Above, Sovereign Grand Commander C. Fred Kleinknecht (center) is pictured with country singer Mel Tillis (left) and Dan Glickman, shortly after Tillis and Glickman were elevated by secret ritual to the coveted 33rd degree of Scottish Rite Freemasonry.

was quoted as saying, "to see such fine public servants as Brother Glickman who exemplify the best of Masonic teachings."[20]

According to *The Scottish Rite Journal,* Glickman's secret Masonic rite in which the coveted degree was conferred was a very special occasion: "Grand Commander C. Fred Kleinknecht, 33rd degree, arranged a special conferral on December 15, 1997, in the Executive Chamber of the House of the Temple."[21] The House of the Temple, in Washington, D.C., is the headquarters and religious center for America's Freemasonry.

"The stage is set for the restructuring of America to begin in earnest within days after the food shortage crisis is acknowledged by the public. Once things are set in motion via Executive Orders, America will be thoroughly transformed into a dictatorship and merged into the global order, the New Civilization."

❧ 10 ❧

Darkness Descending—
Panic, Solutions, and the
Restructuring of America

When the plug is pulled on our economy, all things financial will begin to move southward at a rapid pace. Within days will come reports of food shortages in different areas of the United States. These reports will intensify until the people as a whole panic and rush *enmasse* to foodstores, cleaning them out and emptying shelves. The situation thereafter will not get any better because, shortly after the barren foodstores have locked their doors, word will get out that little or no additional food is going to be forthcoming. The media, in sobering tones, will report that the President and his White House advisors and cabinet are holding nonstop emergency sessions trying to figure out what to do to resolve the food shortage dilemma.

From this point, the prospects for improvement will grow ever dimmer, with the people growing more frustrated by the day. Riots will break out in cities, instigated and led at first by welfare recipients in the ghetto furious because their food stamps are worthless. Many cities will have entire blocks of buildings burned to the ground—especially grocery stores— as ghetto dwellers vent their anger and issue demands for the government to immediately gratify their hunger pangs.

The angry revolt will soon move out to the suburbs and small towns. But whether people turn to violence or not— and the majority will refrain—the demands on the federal, state, and local governments to get the food chain moving and to jump-start the broken economy will escalate until, finally, the politicians and governmental bureaucrats do, indeed, move in a dramatic way. In actuality, this will be the moment for which the Illuminati elite have long awaited.

This is that "moment of critical instability" which will engender revolutionary change and give the Illuminati the opportunity to apply the kind of solutions that, once and for all, will mean the total makeover of society. As long as people were prosperous and contented, they abhorred and rejected change. Now, at last, the middle class and poor alike will not just tolerate change, they will *demand it!*

Ten Programs to Restructure America and the World

Then, in rapid-fire succession, recalling the energetic first 100 days of the Roosevelt Administration, will come programs designed to drastically restructure the economy, adjust the living conditions of all citizens, and restore order out of chaos. The government will take action on these broad fronts:

1. A national computerized I.D. card system will be implemented.

2. Full and complete gun registration will be required. (Later, all guns and firearms in private hands will simply be outlawed and confiscated.)

3. Cash, or currency, will be banned. A number and mark system will be instituted, required of all citizens to buy or sell.

4. Farmers and ranchers will be ordered to share assets in common and to join farm production collectives.

5. A *World Environmental Authority (WEA)* will be set up and granted vast powers to evict farmers, ranchers, and other citizens from their farms and homes to protect nature and sustain the ecosystem.

6. A *World Food Authority (WFA)* will be given control of existing food supplies and have authority over all food production, storage, and distribution.

7. *Federal Emergency Management Agency (FEMA)* detention camps will be activated, to house rioters, food hoarders, resisters and other potential lawbreakers. Many people will appear to have vanished or disappeared as the government conducts night raids, rounding up antigovernment protesters and other suspected "malcontents."

8. The *International Criminal Court (ICC)* will be empowered to hear cases of criminal conduct across all national boundaries, especially the cases of "criminals" accused of food hoarding and resisters to the emerging New Civilization.

9. The *United Nations Educational, Social, and Cultural Organization (UNESCO)* will be empowered to monitor the media (including Christian and patriot media) to insure that newsletters, magazines, television, movies, radio, the internet, etc., contribute positively to "helping the people

understand why all these drastic changes are necessary." UNESCO will also establish approved "core curricula" for public and private schools.

10. Essential sectors and elements of the economy will be nationalized and placed under federal authority until the emergency crisis has passed, to include communications, transportation, postal services, electric power and utilities, fuels, and food.

Executive Orders For a Police State

To calm and appease the frightened, hungry public and to implement the draconian Socialist/Fascist police state, all that's necessary is that the President rule through the issuance of *Executive Orders*. Indeed, Executive Orders already on the books can provide us with a detailed roadmap of where the President and his elitist superiors are going to take America.

Executive Orders are, on their very face, unconstitutional. They bypass the constitutionally required method of enacting legislation—passage by a majority in the House and Senate and signature approval of the President. For many decades now, tracing all the way back to President Abraham Lincoln, presidents have illegally issued Executive Orders, with the administrative and executive branch of government treating them as if they are legitimate laws, binding on the citizenry.

It is simply staggering to realize that the Federal Bureau of Investigation (FBI) was formed under an Executive Order by president Theodore Roosevelt on July 26, 1908. In 1933, President Franklin D. Roosevelt used Executive orders to close all the banks and confiscate all gold held in private hands. The Federal Emergency Management Agency (FEMA) was created by President Jimmy Carter under Executive Order 12148 in 1979 and only belatedly was legislation passed by Congress eight years later to confirm Carter's presidential fiat.

In recent years, especially since FDR, more and more,

presidents have decided to use the route of Executive Orders either to bypass Congress entirely or to speed up the process of wielding governmental powers. President Clinton has been the most flagrant violator; calculating and arrogant, the imperial Mr. Clinton has issued Executive Order after Executive Order. As a result, the United States is now ruled direct from the White House and the stage is set for the restructuring of America to begin in earnest within days after the food shortage crisis is acknowledged by the public. Once things are set in motion via Executive Orders, America will be thoroughly transformed into a dictatorship and merged into the global order, the New Civilization.

Among the Executive Orders already in existence providing for control of peoples' everyday lives and seizure of private property are the following:

E.O. 13010—Seizure of the "Critical Infrastructure." Seizure of computer systems, the internet, satellite systems and telephone and communications systems, by the federal government. Empowerment of the U.S. Armed Forces to perform the functions of government in event of national emergency.

E.O. 10995—Seizure of the communications media.

E.O. 10997—Seizure of all electric power and utility systems, fuels, and minerals.

E.O. 10998—Seizure of all food supplies and resources and all farms and farm equipment.

E.O. 10999 and **E.O. 11005**—Seizure of all means of transportation, including company and personal cars, trucks, trains, airlines, river and ocean vessels, and vehicles and conveyances of any kind, and control over all highways, waterways, and air routes.

E.O. 11000—Mandatory induction of any and all American workers for government projects or missions, placing the entire U.S. work force under the federal government.

E.O. 11001—Seizure of all health, education, and welfare facilities and equipment.

E.O. 11002—Empowers the Postmaster General to register

all U.S.A. men, women, and children and to issue a national I.D. card.

E.O. 11004—Seizure of all housing and finances and the power to direct the relocation of people and resources into designated communities.

E.O. 11051—Empowers the Federal Emergency Management Agency (FEMA) with the authority to independently put Executive Orders into effect in event of increased international tension or economic, financial, or military crises.

E.O. 13083—Centralizes all government powers and authority—national, state, and local—in the federal government. Overrides the 10th Amendment to the U.S. Constitution and makes all state and local laws and regulations subservient and inferior to those of the federal government. Also empowers the federal government to control the social and religious behavior of the people by stating that federal law shall "define the moral, political, and legal character of their lives."

This hideously sinister Executive Order (13083), issued May 14, 1998 by President Clinton, undoubtedly is the most shocking of all. It totally undermines and destroys the Bill of Rights and gives the federal government the awesome power even to define the "moral character" of peoples' lives! As Bob Trefz states in his Christian magazine, *Cherith Chronicle*, this incredible Executive Order literally makes government "supreme over the human conscience."[1]

Trefz, notes that the 10th Amendment actually severely *restricts and limits* the federal government, reserving powers "to the states respectively, or to the people." This is why, said Trefz, the President's action in issuing Executive Order 13083 was so diabolically insidious:

Federal law, in all its enormous octopus of hundreds of thousands of pages, is asserted in this Executive Order as... (having) absolute supremacy over the moral character of the individual's life. In other words, the federal government holds the place of God in defining morality. The same holds true in the political and legal spheres.

This does not sound like the intent of the framers of the Constitution who dreaded such a thing ever happening, doing all in their power to prohibit it. They placed federal law *subject* to the Constitution, *not on a par with it.* This limited power of the federal government was to be checked by the sovereign power of the people and the states...

The Bill of Rights defined the zone of unalienable individual rights that the federal government has no authority over. It is on this battlefield of the destruction of these unalienable rights that the war wages to destroy those unalienable rights and assert federal authority over the soul in those areas that lie between the soul and God Almighty alone.[2]

Patriots Cause An Uproar

Though the general public was told little or nothing about this Executive Order horror by either the media or their representatives in the Congress, in 1998 a small group of determined patriots caused an uproar about this Stalinist-oriented infringement on the peoples' rights and liberties. On the internet and on radio talk shows they complained with a mighty voice. Amazingly, possibly because the biannual federal election for the Congress was only a few months away, the Congress moved quickly to nullify Executive Order 13083.

But the Illuminati and their puppets in the White House and elsewhere in the political realm could not let this rest. Executive Order 13083 is far too valuable to their hidden plan for dictatorship. Shortly after the November 1998 elections, the White House announced that the President intended to reissue the nullified Executive Order. To garner political support for their unconscionable rebuff of the people and the Congress, the President and his Illuminati overlords moved the battle to the states. On November 14, 1998, *World Net Daily,* a global news service published on the World Wide Web, carried this astonishing news article:

The National Governors Association would like to have a national ID system, and plans to work with the White House to reinstate Executive Order 13083 to make that a reality.

The bipartisan NGA (National Governors Assoc.)... plans to help craft a revised version of the order that will alter the relationship between states and the federal government.

An internal document used by the NGA to inform all governors of their goals and objectives was made available to WorldNetDaily, along with a "Fact Sheet on Federalism" used by the White House staff. Both documents were provided by a Republican source.

Each document shows that both the White House, and the nation's Governors, plan to put the currently suspended executive order into effect.

One of the main reasons for the alteration of state and federal government relations is to provide for "preemption of state and local laws" by the federal government, according to the NGA document.

The act also calls for digitized biometric information to be a part of each person's national ID license, or "smart card." The biometric information will include fingerprints, retina scans, DNA prints, and other similar information.

The bottom line is that the new order would wreak havoc on the balance of power envisioned by the Constitution between the States and the federal government.[3]

State Governors Agree to Trash Constitution

Here we have a disturbing, mind-boggling precedent—the 50 governors of the states actually coming together and agreeing to trash the Constitution, to decimate the people's precious historical heritage of freedom and liberty against federal encroachment, and to turn over all *governing power* throughout America to the absolute rulers of the federal government. Let it be recorded for posterity that the coming era of terror and tyranny was birthed first in the hallowed inner sanctum of the Illuminati elite, then codified by Executive Order of the President of the United States, and, finally, confirmed by the governors of the 50 states acting as a unified body under the auspices of the Rockefeller-founded National Governors Association. Let it further be said that darkness has descended upon America with the full consent of the states.

Almost as ominous was the fact that at the exact moment the governors were jointly acting in November, 1998 to cede all power and authority to the President to dictatorially rule America by Executive Order, a move to impeach President Clinton fizzled out after Republican conservatives in the Congress were beaten down by liberal Democrats and "moderate" Republicans. The message was made clear: The President, though he be a proven perjurer and lawbreaker, reigns supreme. No one can stop him. The foundation has, therefore, been set for a Hitlerian grab of virtually unimaginable proportions.

In the perilous days ahead, as the dread specter of famine hits home, we can expect the President to radically reorient and reorganize society in a cosmic fashion. A first step will be an order issued to effect the *collectivization* of farming. Both Stalin and Mao Tse Tung accomplished this in their respective nations. Now, collectivization shall be mandated for America and, indeed, for the whole world. Since the U.S.A. is the world's only superpower, all the nations of the world will look to this country for leadership during the coming food crisis. In effect, the President of the U.S.A. will also be President of Earth.

When Humanity Comes of Age

The agenda outlining this collectivization process was explained in some detail in two key books, *When Humanity Comes of*

Age and *The Initiation of the World*, by Englishwoman and New Age planner, Vera Stanley Alder.

First published in Great Britain by The Aquarian Press, these two books are used as handbooks by those intent on fostering a One World Government. They have been reprinted repeatedly in the United States, being most recently published and distributed by Samuel Weiser, Inc., a New York publisher specializing in occult publications. Samuel Weiser displays on these books as a company logo the Egyptian ankh, a perverted cross which has as its uppermost focal point the Satanic circle. Also on the cover of *When Humanity Comes of Age* is an evil-looking serpent coiled around a white dove and a drawing of the Egyptian Sphinx.

When Humanity Comes of Age provides an incredible blueprint for the New World Order, described as the "Divine Plan" or "Ideal World Plan." This Divine Plan is said to have derived from the lessons humanity has learned "through a long series of incarnations upon earth," and from the "wisdom" which Alder claims can be found in the ancient Mystery Teachings. These lessons, Alder explains, reveal that man is ready for a Golden Age to begin:

> The ancient writings all claim that a Golden Age is indeed due to follow the death of the present Dark Age.

> It seems unquestionable that a time has now arrived in history where an attempt to rebuild civilization will—and must be made... Plans and hope for world reconstruction are now universal and permeate all strata of the community.[4]

A Cashless Society

According to Alder, The Divine Plan calls for a cashless society. Currency will be obsolete as a new system is implemented:

> Economics will be founded on a quite different basis from

that of the present capitalistic system. A system of exchange between peoples of goods and services will, when intelligently developed, gradually cancel out the need for buying and selling with money.[5]

Echoing Alder, Lucis Trust founder Alice Bailey, in her book, *Externalization of the Hierarchy,* writes of a great world leader to come. Because this leader will have authority over the world's money and finances, the euphemism, the *"adjuster of finances,"* is used to describe him:

> When the *adjuster of finances* (as an advanced disciple from this Ashram is called in the Hierarchy) appears, he will find conditions greatly changed from those now prevalent and this to the following extent:
>
> 1. The principle of barter and exchange (to the benefit of all concerned) will control.
>
> 2. National currencies will have been largely superseded, not only by a system of barter but by a universal monetary exchange.[6]

Food, Gold, and Silver to be Controlled or Owned by State

If Alder's detailed blueprint is carried out, *food* will be closely controlled by a *World Food Authority.* Banking and monetary rules would be globally standardized, and gold, silver, and other precious metals would be seized from individual owners. A universal currency would also be issued and a new marking and identification system used for purchases made:

> Agricultural surpluses will be passed through a "Central Surplus Pool," controlled by the Council For Economics. There would be no need for a paper currency, nor even for the retention of gold, silver, and other precious metals by

individuals or countries. Money as such would revert to its original token value. As the bulk of commerce would be carried on by the means of exchange, and individual needs would be supplied on a ration card system, the need for the handling of money would dwindle...

There would be a central bank which decided the value or price cheaply in terms of labor and quality of all good produced. This value would probably be described in terms of letters and numbers, the letters representing the quality of work in material and the numbers representing the hours of work entailed.[7]

One World Government and a President of Earth

Vera Stanley Alder carefully prescribes a system to be set up whereby there will be a *One World Government* with a *Council For Economics* that reports to the *President of Earth,* known simply as the World Leader. According to Alder, "The principles of world government...should insist on the right of every man to the necessities of life."[8] She says that the *Council for Economics* would see to the just redistribution of resources so that all will be shared in common.

It is scary to read Alder's dark comments in her chapter, "From Self-Mastery to World Service." She proclaims that the supreme goal of the coming World Order will be to achieve the "oneness and the interdependence of humanity," with its motto being *The greatest good for the greatest number.*[9]

In other words, individual rights will be stamped out as the elite decides what is in the best interest of all humanity. Alder's sly use of the phrase, "The greatest good for the greatest number," is the same slogan and motto used by Communists Marx and Lenin and such modern-day organizations as the Lucis Trust, the Tara Center, World Goodwill, and many other front organizations set up by occultists and the Illuminati.

Model Collectives—Communitarianism

To achieve this Socialist utopian goal of "the greatest good for the greatest number," the elite have come up with a new ideology—*Communitarianism.* President Clinton, say news reports, has fully endorsed this new ideological concept. It calls for the collectivization of all people and all assets as "community property," held in common. As Hillary Clinton, the First Lady, explains in her acclaimed (by liberals) book, *It Takes a Village,* children are also owned as chattel property by the whole community and not by parents alone.

The Communitarianism framework is necessary to justify the forced collectivization of society. The concept is often found in recent New Age teachings, most of which align perfectly with Marxist and Soviet ideology. Hillary's book, *It Takes a Village,* is only one example of the Communitarian propaganda being spewed out with regularity in books, newspapers, magazines, movies, and on television. The John Lennon song, "Imagine," epitomized the Communitarian strategy for the reorganization of the world.

The supremacy of the group, of the whole, over the individual and his rights is paramount in Communitarianism. Virginia Essene, in the popular New Age book, *New Teachings for an Awakened Humanity,* writes:

> We now enter a period wherein the goal of individual
> salvation is no longer appropriate. Our guidance calls for
> a collective transformation.[10]

M. Scott Peck, whose books such as *The Road Less Traveled* have sold over ten million copies, is another popular guru for the rising Communitarian philosophy. Peck heads up a foundation whose goal is to foster "Community." In *A Different Drum: Community Making and Peace,* he states the Communitarian position in stark, almost fanatical, terms. One can imagine either Peck or another true believer like him—perhaps the coming President of Earth—proclaiming someday in the future, to an anxious and embattled global citizenry on the brink of starvation, these very words of M. Scott Peck from his book:

> In and through Community lies the salvation of the world. Nothing is more important...For the human race today stands at the brink of self-annihilation...I'm scared for my own skin. I'm even more scared for this skin of my children and I'm scared for your skins. I want to save your skin. I need you, and you need me, for salvation. We must come into Community with each other.[11]

Reorganizing Our Farms and Small Town America

The resettlement of farmers, ranchers, and small town residents will be accomplished using the framework of *Communitarianism.* In my own earlier book, *America Shattered,* I provided an extensive examination of what the elite plans for America in attaining the goals of Communitarianism. I explained that the best description of this future vision is found in Vera Stanley Alder's classic book, *When Humanity Comes of Age.* Let us, therefore, revisit my analysis of Alder's blueprint for the coming days of restructuring and reorganization of the farming sector and of small town America.

First, Alder says that the federal government, following the dictates of Executive Orders and directives from the United Nations (to be the center for the One World Government), will establish a *Town and Country Planning Council* to oversee and supervise the restructuring of communities across America. Perfectly designed resettlement collectives will be set up in isolated areas, and "people will be encouraged" to move to the new "Model Communities."[12]

When I first read Alder's supposedly glowing description of the organization of the proposed Model Communities, shivers went up and down my spine. Each Community, Alder explains, will be self-contained. There will be one, massive, unified complex of buildings, all interconnected, with everything from medical and health facilities to cultural and recreation centers and schools. There will be "a single Community meals center," or cafeteria, where all families will eat in common. The Community will have just *one* church because everyone will have one faith—the New Age World Religion. The same building used for the church will be used to house the courts and the police.[13]

In her book, Alder even includes a drawing of this post-Depression ideal Community. One glance at her dream world, fantasy utopia should be enough to shake up anyone who has not had their minds blinded by Satan. *Alder's blueprint for the ideal Community resembles an architect's plan for a prison, a gulag, or a concentration camp.*

Indeed, Alder's vision is reminiscent of what was actually in practice at Jim Jones' Peoples Temple "paradise" in Guyana. It resembles the Nazis' forced labor camps, Pol Pot's *Khmer Rhouge* farm collectives, and the resettlement villages built and operated by the U.S. Armed Forces to "pacify" and house Vietnamese in Vietnam and the Meskito Indians in Nicaragua.

The Family Collective

In the architect's sketch, or drawing, for Alder's "perfect," future Community, there are no doors or exits to the outside, external world. There is no escape route, and traffic is not allowed to move freely in and out of the Community. The only entrance and exit are by use of a ribbon train/rail system that looks suspiciously like a serpent in its construction.

In the ideal Community, kids will not be able to play freely outdoors; they and their parents are forced to use whatever playground facilities are provided on the rooftops of the common buildings.

It should not be assumed that city dwellers and those in suburbia will be spared the rigors and horrors of collectivization. The Plan includes *all* of America and the world. Community cells will be established in urban areas and in the suburbs. There will be industrial as well as agricultural communes. As Bill Clinton has stated, the objective is to reorganize the whole world.

*This illustration, which came straight out of her book, **When Humanity Comes of Age,** pictures Vera Stanley Adler's vision of the ideal collectivist community for farms and small towns, as proposed for the coming New Civilization. Does this look to you like a home...or a concentration camp?*

The proposed Community for the coming New Age of economic restoration is, in reality, obviously a prison and a confinement center where families will live as hostages, as indebted prisoners and locked-up slaves of their captors. The shocking truth is that Alder's ideal Community is a warmed over version of Communist China and Soviet Russia's "ideal" family collective. This becomes painfully apparent when we read Alder's dictum that: "Collective agriculture and collective industrial work should be the rule."[14]

A World Food Authority

The Illuminist-led bureaucrats have decided that the people of America have too much food and too many goods—and the remainder of the world's population has too few. According to the proposed Model Community regulations, food and agricultural surpluses will, therefore, be turned into a *Surplus Pool* and redistributed to other areas of the world where the need is greater. Naturally, there will be a *World Food Authority* in charge of this redistribution.

The embryo of this World Food Authority (WFA) is already found in the United Nations current *World Food and Agriculture Organization (WFAO)*. After the hunger crunch impacts, the powers of the WFAO will be vastly increased and a new, more simple and streamlined name given this global body—WFA.

Hoarding to be Prohibited

One of the most pressing and immediate concerns of the WFA will be to stop and prevent the hoarding of so-called "excess food" by Americans, Europeans, and the people of other formerly wealthy nations. Not surprisingly, the politicians and bureaucrats who head the WFA will have a model law handy and ready to use in shaping their global guidelines outlawing hoarding.

As far back as 1950, the U.S. Congress passed legislation prohibiting hoarding in event of declared emergencies. In 1951, this law was strengthened and on June 25, 1974, Executive Order 1179 further expanded the authority of the federal government in this regard. A reading of the law makes clear that the President or his representatives may, at their discretion, forcibly confiscate food, fuel, or any other material they deem as excess to your immediate need. Here is the wording of Section 2072 of the War and National Defense Production Act of 1950, chapter 932, statute 798:

Sec. 2072. Hoarding of designated scarce materials. In order to prevent hoarding, no person shall accumulate (1) in excess of the reasonable demands of business, personal, or home consumption, or (2) for the purpose of resale at prices in excess of prevailing market prices, materials which have been designated by the President as scarce materials or materials the supply of which would be threatened by such accumulation. The president shall order published in the *Federal Register,* and in such other manner as he may deem appropriate, every designation of material the accumulation of which is unlawful and any withdrawal of such designation.

In making such designations the President may prescribe such conditions with respect to the accumulation of materials in excess of the reasonable demands of business, personal, or home consumption as he deems necessary to carry out the objectives of this Act (sections 2061 to 2171 of this Appendix). This section shall not be construed to limit the authority contained in sections 101 of this Act (sections 2071 and 2154 of this Appendix) (Sept. 8, 1950, ch. 932, title 1, Sec. 102, 64 Stat. 799; July 31, 1951, ch. 275, title 1, Sec. 101(b), 65 Stat. 132.) AMENDMENTS.

Seamless Authoritarian Control

The World Food Authority will work closely with a multitude

of other globalist groups and organizations to assume a seamless, authoritarian control over all aspects of food production, storage, distribution, and rationing. The North American Free Trade Agreement (NAFTA) organization, the World Trade Organization (WTO), the European Economic Community (EEC), and the International Standards Organization (ISO) are existing organizations that wield great power. For example:

☐ John G. Gordon, writing in *Veritas* newspaper (July, 1996), says that, "rules enforced by the WTO made it illegal for the U.S. to retain sufficient supplies of grain for emergencies. The U.S. was compelled to sell our grain reserves to the rest of the world...The sad reality of all this is that Americans in the land which feeds the world over 80 percent of its food could actually starve to death while the rest of the world eats."[15]

☐ A 1998 United Nations treaty on migratory fish stocks now dictates where fishermen can fish, the types and quantity of fish and quantity that can be caught, and which nations can fish for which variety of fish. This prompted an e-mail writer to bitterly complain: "As a commercial fisherman now under control of the United Nation's treaty on migratory fish stocks, I am angry. Who on Earth gave these people the right to control our food source?"

☐ ISO 9000 standards begin to go into effect starting in 1999, requiring uniform, minimum standards of quality in every industry on Earth. So far, 150 nations have signed up to comply with ISO standards. Beginning in the year 2000, no one can sell a widget or thingamajig of any kind unless their production facility, factory, or mill is ISO 9000 certified according to standards of the International Standards Organization.[16] As one top industry expert attests:

Government agencies are adopting the ISO 9000 standards as their own quality system standards. The U.S. Department of Defense (DOD), NATO, and the FDA have all announced their intention to adopt ISO 9000, *possibly with some additional requirements.*[17]

The bureaucrats of WTO, EEC, and ISO are now laboring to publish tens of thousands of pages of complex regulations detailing the minimum standards of acceptability for every food crop and industrial product. If a farmer's products do not meet these standards—and believe me, when the ISO 9000 program is fully implemented, his products will undergo strenuous quality inspections—they must be destroyed, no matter how edible they may be. The standards have little or no relationship to health, safety needs, or similar requirements.

An e-mail I received from Denmark elaborates on what is going on in Europe and will soon be customary here in America. Under EEC rules, said the e-mail writer, "we get all kinds of silly restrictions like—all eggs have to be the same size, and cucumbers have to be relatively straight. Forty-two pages of regulations exist explaining to farmers the standard requirements for cucumbers—the degree of curve allowable, their weight, color, feel, texture, and so on. Most of these rules are petty but seem intended to demand uniformity, diminishing the varieties of nature."

In *The Daily Telegraph,* a major daily newspaper in Great Britain, we read further of just how powerful is the European Union's "Common Agricultural Policy:"

EUROPE PAYS TO LET FOOD ROT

Nearly three million tons of fruit and vegetables, including almost a million tons of apples, were destroyed in 1993, at a cost of £439 million (AUD$900 million), under the European Union's Common Agricultural Policy.

More than 720,000 tons of peaches, over half a million tons of oranges and 165,000 tons of nectarines were also taken off the market by farmers paid by Brussels to destroy their own produce.

British taxpayers alone paid £57 million (AUD $120 million) towards the cost of destroying fruit and vegetables

of almost every type grown in Europe. All were fit for
human consumption.

Here you have a scheme whereby European taxpayers are
funding a scheme which keeps the price of fruit and
vegetables artificially high by destroying perfectly good
produce.

The fruit is destroyed by being buried in the ground and
allowed to rot.[18]

Implanted Biochips to Keep Track of Animals and People

Farm animals, too, come under the scrutiny of the food
regulations. In *The European* newspaper recently was an eye-
opening piece about a new EEC project to attach electronic
tags to every one of Europe's estimated 300 million farm animals. The first one million are now being tagged. Later, if this
works, microchips will be inserted in *all* the animals' bodies:

Veterinarians across six countries of the European Union
have begun the process of attaching electronic tags to
nearly a million animals.

The Commission's research centre is contributing more
than Ecu 10 million ($11m) to the cause, which it says
will reduce fraudulent claims for funds from the Common
Agricultural Policy.

The electronic tags are a technological generation or three
more advanced than the cowboys' old techniques of
branding or cutting a notch out of a calf's ear. Your ewe,
cow or goat is to be given a choice of three fetching
styles: an ear-tag, an implant or a stomach tag.

The tags can be read by an antenna from a distance of 80

centimeters at a rate of about 30 animals a minute. In
theory, the tag will be read every time an animal enters or
leaves a farm, is put on or taken off a lorry or is admitted
to a slaughterhouse. (Calves which don't want to be killed
are strongly advised to lose their transponders in the long
grass.)[19]

The final sentences of the above article are chilling in
their implications—electronic tags "*will be read every time
an animal enters or leaves a farm...or is admitted to a
slaughterhouse (calves which don't want to be killed are
strongly advised to lose their transponders in the long
grass*)."

In my highly documented book, *Project L.U.C.I.D.—The
Beast 666 Universal Human Control System,* I proved the
existence of a secret plot by the government to "tag" every
man, woman, and child on Earth with a programmable,
implantable biochip. With all of humanity bearing in their
bodies a computer biochip, the opportunity for government
tyranny will advance exponentially.

Could it not be that someday in the not so distant future—
possibly only a year, two, or three from today—every time
a person enters or leaves a farm, collective, or their home or
apartment in the city, they will be tracked and monitored by
way of an implanted biochip transponder? Since this now
appears a distinct possibility, perhaps we should heed the
sardonic advice given by the writer of the article in *The
European* newspaper to animals who wish to avoid the
slaughterhouse:

"Calves which don't want to be killed are strongly advised
to lose their transponders in the long grass."

> *"If the power of the gospel is not felt throughout the length and breadth of the land, anarchy and misrule, degradation and misery, corruption and darkness, will reign without mitigation or end."*
> —*Daniel Webster*

> *"The marines are undertaking Urban Warrior (military exercise) with the expectation that future wars are, increasingly, likely to be waged on the city streets."*
> —*Major Frank Luster*
> U.S. Marine Corps

❦ 11 ❦

Food Riots, Chaos and Terror— The Collapse of Civilization

A sweeping wave of hunger, alarm, anger, terror, murder, and riot is someday very soon going to overwhelm the United States of America. Each of us will be affected. Indeed, the whole world is going to feel the shock waves. When people everywhere suddenly find themselves without food and with no way to satisfy their intense hunger pains, an explosion of emotions will hit and chaos will break out in every village, town, and city.

While, historically, country after country has suffered famine, America has always been spared. Except for pockets of poverty when families had to go without eating, the masses have always been sufficiently fed, enjoying at least a minimum level of sustenance.

When a person has never before been denied a basic necessity like food, water, or shelter, it is difficult for that person to even imagine that circumstances could change dramatically and suddenly. As Donald McAlvany recently remarked of the American citizenry in his *The McAlvany Intelligence Advisor* newsletter:

> It would seem that they have never been hungry, had their income reduced to nothing, or been in a crisis situation as seen in Los Angeles during the riots in the spring of 1992 or in Jakarta, Indonesia in recent months. Or maybe they just trust in Bill Clinton and FEMA to keep their shelves stocked with food in times of financial, social, or political crisis. Trust is a wonderful thing, but if you're out of food, out of a job, or in a crisis—food reserves may be better.[1]

What is in Store For America?

The crisis that will soon confront us can be expected to take shape along several lines of difficulty. We know that the Holy Bible prophesies famine, pestilence, disease, and other calamities. Any, or all, of these horrendous problems could trigger massive rioting and unbridled violence.

In a major speech on May 6, 1992 reported in both the *New York Times* and the *Associated Press*, former Soviet Union boss Mikhail Gorbachev, now a favored "son" of the Illuminati elite, reeled off a list of several crises-type situations that may compel national governments to yield sovereignty to a global government. These crises, said Gorbachev, would then require adoption of a *global solution*. He mentioned, "The prospect of catastrophic climate changes, more frequent droughts, floods, hunger, epidemics, national-ethnic conflicts, and other similar catastrophes."

Maurice Strong, former Chairman of the United Nations Environmental Program, in a report to the participants of the Earth Summit, held in Rio de Janeiro in 1992, warned that the "environmental crisis," by itself—not even considering other potential crises—will soon cause a strong shift in how humans conduct their lives:

> It is clear that current lifestyles and consumption patterns of the affluent middle-class...involving high meat intake, consumption of large amounts of frozen and "convenience" foods, ownership of motor-vehicles, numerous electric household appliances, home and workplace air-conditioning... expansive suburban housing...are not sustainable.[2]

Please don't think for a moment that billionaire Maurice Strong intends to give up his plush mansions, luxury autos, and sumptuous meals. His comments are intended for the serfs and peasants. When the financial crash and economic hard times bear down on the ordinary citizen, Strong and his associates will no doubt be hunkered down in an underground city somewhere in the U.S.A., Canada, or Europe, smiling and waiting for the smoke to clear. Then, they will step forward with their proposed global solutions to the mounting concerns of the stunned citizenry.

What Might Precipitate the Final Crisis?

One of the principal ways a food shortage can be generated is *adverse severe weather conditions*. Mind-boggling technological developments now make possible the manipulation of weather patterns and the causing of major weather events (tornado, rain, lightening storm, hurricane, typhoon, drought, flood, etc.) by the government. An eye-opening, official

198 ⬜ DAYS OF HUNGER, DAYS OF CHAOS

Department of Defense report authored by seven U.S. Air Force officers in 1996, entitled *"Weather as a Force Multiplier,"* details how "U.S. aerospace forces can own the weather by capitalizing on emerging technologies" which have significant "war-fighting applications." The report states that the capability to wage hostile war with weather modification extends to causing fog, clouds, thunderstorms, and droughts.

Is it a coincidence that weather patterns and events in America in recent years have been wildly erratic, even record-breaking? Larry Acker, publisher of *FFF Forecasts*, an investments and commodities advisory service, remarks that:

> ...It is getting more and more difficult to raise a consistently good crop almost everywhere in the world because the general weather patterns have turned erratic and highly variable...This variable and erratic weather can threaten the world's food supply...[3]

Acker goes on to say that in terms of severe weather, "Some strange things are going to happen...The evidence is building that this may be a 5-year super weather cycle, and it may have a similar effect to the...years of 1815-1820. In that period, 1820 was so dry in the central U.S. that whole species became extinct—especially animals—and it could happen again."[4]

A major war in the Middle East, precipitated by ongoing conflict and bickering between Arabs and Israelis, could break out, escalating to the devastating exchange of nuclear weapons. Israel has at least 200 atomic bombs in its arsenals, probably many more. Israel also has a large number of chemical and biological devices. Arab powers are also endeavoring to develop nuclear, biological, and chemical weapons.

Russia and the U.S.A. have a combined 50,000 nuclear warheads and a significant capability in chemical and biological warfare.

Terrorists are reported to possibly have the potential to obliterate targets with small nukes that can be hidden in suitcases—developed by the old Soviet Union. The CIA (which rarely can be believed) propaganda story is that Arab terrorists also have the ability to deliver and detonate chemical-biological weapons in America's cities.

The Chernobyl incident in Russia, in which a nuclear reactor's core exploded, demonstrates the danger to food supplies of nuclear radiation. Literally hundreds of miles of valuable farmland in Russia were contaminated by radiation from the Chernobyl plant.

Sidney Pollard, author of *Wealth and Poverty: An Economic History of the Twentieth Century*, writes that the ominous Chernobyl nuclear disaster "cast a pall" over crop growers and retailers. "Buyers could never be sure of the source of their fruits and vegetables," said Pollard, "They could never be certain purchases had not been contaminated by nuclear fallout." [5]

Plagues (pestilence) are highly possible as killers of crops, whether purposely spread by governments or naturally occurring. Due to mad cow disease, all cows and beef cattle in Great Britain were destroyed. History could repeat itself and American beef cattle could all be afflicted with a destructive virus. Biological weapons that employ deadly anthrax now in the arsenals of the U.S.A. and Russia are proven killers of cattle—and people.

Wildlife as a potential source of meat may also be affected. R.E. McMaster, in his excellent *The Reaper* newsletter, reported that, "Wildlife in the Rocky Mountain region, particularly elk and deer, are being afflicted with Chronic Wasting Disease (CWD), a mysterious ailment that attacks elk and deer, causing them to become listless and languid." McMaster reports that CWD is always fatal and that, "The infected animal literally wastes away, starving to death for no apparent reason."[6]

Whatever it is that generates the coming, severe food shortages, it is a surety that America has practically no reserves. For decades our nation maintained a standing reserve of cheese, butter, grains and other foodstuffs available to us in time of crises. No longer. Several years ago, President Clinton either sold at less than market prices or gave away those reserves to foreign countries. As a consequence, America has on hand at any given time at best 30 days of food supplies. But even at that, this food may not make it to retail grocery stores. The vulnerable trucking and railroad distribution system could break down, leaving people destitute with no more than three or four days of stock level in local supermarkets and stores.

Earth Filled With Violence

When the foreboding, sudden emergency arrives, the world's economy will immediately grind to a halt. Banks and stock brokerages will close, food and hardware stores will be emptied of food and other essentials within days. Factories and offices will announce temporary closures. Transportation lines will be blocked, electrical power and water may be disrupted, and most communications media will cease broadcasting. Panic will set in as people sit in solitude in their homes and apartments, wondering what steps to take and contemplating on their futures.

However, this early period of shock and contemplation will not last long. Soon, surprise and consternation will give way to a spasm of extreme violence and corruption. The world will return to the wicked and bloody situation it was in the days before the great flood recorded in the Biblical book of *Genesis*, to wit:

And God saw that the wickedness of man was great in the earth, and that every imagination of the thoughts of his heart was only evil continually...The earth also was corrupt before God, and the earth was filled with violence. (*Genesis 6:5,11*)

The Earth, says the Bible, was corrupt and "filled with violence" in Noah's day. Now, pay attention to this: Jesus our Lord prophesied that, "...as the days of Noah were, so shall also the coming of the Son of Man be." (*Matthew 24:37*)

Christ said that people in the days of Noah were eating,

drinking, and marrying—ignorantly thinking that the world would continue as it had—"And knew not until the flood came, and took them all away; so shall also the coming of the Son of Man be." (*Matthew 24:38-39*)

Jesus' prophecy reveals to us that just before His return, it will be on Earth as it was in the days of Noah. We are going to experience days of distress and violence of unimaginable proportions never seen. America will suffer a veritable *flood* of violence that will engulf the whole nation.

What will a debauched, immoral and ungodly people—as now populate America—do, once they get over their initial shock and denial? Who can doubt that many will be so angry and mean-spirited in being denied, they will initiate a wild spree of looting, burning, and rioting?

A Bloody Historical Parallel?

During the 18th century French Revolution, it is reported that troubled messengers to the Royal Court lamented to Queen Marie Antoinette, "Your highness, the people are hungry. They haunt the streets in desperation, begging for crumbs. They have no bread."

"Then, let them eat cake," said Marie Antoinette.

The guillotines soon flowed with blood. The Queen and King were among the first to feel the swift blade on their necks. Mobs pillaged churches, ravaged homes, and tortured and killed with utter abandon. Red-stained rivers were full of rotting, bloated bodies.

When a man is hungry, he cares little for decency and goodness. His stomach groans in despair. His body aches in misery. His mind is impaired. He expected to be fed. Now he is starving and desperate. Who knows what he will do in exchange for relief?

Don McAlvany, in *The McAlvany Intelligence Advisor*, comments:

With the vast majority of the U.S. population now residing

in cities and suburbs, most people have very little idea where food comes from or how it is processed and distributed. It's simply assumed that a cornucopia of microwave meals, meats, produce and baked goods appear magically at the local supermarket every day.[7]

However, no longer will food magically appear. The undisciplined masses will be furious. Panic will set in. Mobs will vent their anger, and this will mean even less an opportunity for food to show up locally:

What if riots broke out in New York, Los Angeles, Detroit, Miami, etc.? Truckers would refuse to haul cargo through bombed or burned out war zones—remember what happened to trucker Reginald Denny during the 1992 LA riots?—and city residents would go hungry. Hardcore welfare types, indoctrinated with a "government-owes-me-a-living" mentality, would loot stores and warehouses, and anyone who didn't stock up before the chaos would be on an involuntary fast.[8]

The inner city ghettos will erupt with gunfire and bloodshed. Commercial buildings and government housing complexes will be torched. But that won't net the depraved mobs any food. Thus, the looting and commotion will move out to the suburbs where armed (if they are smart) home owners will be forced to defend their homes and material possessions, their families, and whatever food and water they have remaining.

Fiendish Acts Programmed to Occur

Keep in mind that millions of young people in recent years were raised on satanic heavy metal music, taught that traditional morality and religious values mean little, fed a diet of sick, fiendish movies like *The Texas Chain Saw Massacre, Jason,* and *Friday the 13th*, and introduced to drugs, alcohol, and perverted sex. Many are taught by the public schools to love and esteem themselves. The social system encourages youth to disrespect, revile and hate their parents and to despise anyone in authority.

Now comes the deluge—the flood of evildoing brought about by mass hunger and deprivation. Can you honestly say that this apathetic, dumbed-down, lustful, demented generation—and I am talking about not only the youthful, so-called "Generation X" but also a hundred million or more Americans coming into adulthood since the New Age, Hippie, India guru era of the 60s and 70s—can keep from committing indecent, murderous acts of violence to satisfy their physical hunger pangs and quiet the inner fear they experience? These are men, women, and youth who have been culturally conditioned by the media to blaspheme Jesus Christ, seduced by TV producers to practice sorcery as they view Saturday morning cartoons, and taught by liberal clergy to imagine that worship of Buddha, Krishna, Mohammed, Allah, and spirit ancestors is just as worthy as paying homage to the living God in heaven (whom most do not believe exists!).

Woe to this generation of foulmouthed profaners when the bad times hit home. They shall kill and be killed in continuous bloody episodes of terror and defilement. Even then, most will refuse to repent. Instead, this generation of lost Americans will revel in their sordid deeds, and violence will rise to greater heights than any time in the annals of human history, filling up the Earth with violence and corruption just as in the days of Noah:

> And the rest of the men which were not killed by these plagues yet repented not of the works of their hands, that they should not worship devils, and idols of gold, and silver, and brass, and stone, and of wood: which neither can see, nor hear, nor walk:
>
> Neither repented they of their murders, nor of their sorceries, nor of their fornication, nor of their thefts. (*Revelation 9:20-21*)

Specter of Blood and Death

Jesus warned that before the final, climatic explosion of history, there would be birth pangs felt—much as happens to a woman nearing delivery of her child. Tremors occur before an earthquake, fiery plumes of smoke and rumblings just prior to a volcanic eruption. So, too, are we feeling the first vibrations of the coming great crisis.

Riots, looting, and bloody murders due to economic implosion and famine have occurred in Africa and Asia. We should heed these occurrences as early warning signs of an approaching world catastrophe:

☐ In 1997 and 1998, currency speculators, egged on by the Illuminati elite, collapsed the economies of Asia. Rioting and bloodshed broke out in the Philippines, Indonesia, and elsewhere. In Indonesia, the world's fifth most populous country, chaos reigned supreme. Marchers clashed with riot police and soldiers in the capitol city of Jakarta. In cities everywhere, Moslem plunderers raided the homes and apartments of Christians, killing the men and raping and torturing women. A reported mob of 125,000 such thugs assembled.[9]

☐ On August 25, 1997, on international shortwave radio, it was reported that, "In Southeast China, government purchasers were in a rural town buying the local crops when one farmer realized that the scales of the officials were short by 30 percent. An argument ensued which was quickly followed by a full-scale riot involving 1,000 farmers who hurled bricks and stones at the government men, driving then out of town. They later returned with 400 paramilitary troops to restore order by arresting 30 farmers and offering a 30 percent increase in payments."[10]

☐ In Russia in early September, 1998, lengthening lines of nervous but surly citizens waited for banks to open their doors. Often, depositors would scramble and break out in fistcuffs trying to get ahead of one another, fearful that the banks would run out of money. Simultaneously, mobs of frightened women and older citizens cleaned out food stores and marketplaces, paying with dollars because no merchant would accept the devalued, sinking Russian ruble. Burglaries and break-ins of homes and businesses were rampant, and it was reported that, "The hottest theft item in Russia is food."[11]

The Western press began to sound alarms that an angry and frustrated Russian populace might seek a revisit of the 1917 revolution, either to return the Communists to power or to install hardcore Russian nationalists to the Kremlin.[12]

□ In North Korea in late 1998, it was reported that over 3.5 million people had died of starvation since 1994. Government troops were called to guard collective farms and plantations and ward off hungry people. One reliable source stated:

> The rate of death from starvation in some regions is about 27 percent. People report that every night trucks drive around the villages to pick up the corpses, which are then buried in common graves.

> Because of the food shortages, the army keeps guards at plantation sites. Hungry people often raid the crops before the state workers start picking the produce. But the posting of guards is not always effective because the soldiers, hungry themselves, are easily bribed with offers of the stolen products. Even the farmers with secret fields in the highlands must guard their crops before the harvest.

> Experts say the city dwellers survive only thanks to a system of public distribution, and that even among the "privileged ones" the pangs of hunger are beginning to be felt.[13]

America has so far been an oasis of tranquility in a desert of world despair. But our time is coming. When it does, our federal government, now run behind-the-scenes by unseen forces, will quickly take advantage of the mounting social instability:

Urban riots, a major war, or widespread economic calamity
would provide a power-hungry federal government with a
perfect excuse to impose executive orders and stringent
controls on the food supply, food deliveries, so-called food
rationing, etc. National rationing was imposed during
World War II and a thriving, "unofficial" or black market,
emerged. But the situation would be far worse today.[14]

United Nations Troops to Intervene in United States Turmoil

To quell the growing unrest and restore law and order,
Washington D.C. will request the United Nations to intervene,
contending that the depleted National Guardsmen and the
sapped strength of the U.S. Armed Forces (many servicemen
are toiling in Bosnia, the Persian Gulf, and in 75 other assorted
countries overseas) require international help from the UN's
blue-helmeted "peacekeepers."

Following the Los Angeles riots in 1992, Henry Kissinger
stated, "Today Americans would be outraged if UN troops
entered Los Angeles to restore order; tomorrow they will be
grateful."[15]

Now we understand why President Clinton supported the
UN's proposed global taxation plan, with a UN equivalent
of our IRS to collect taxes from United States and world
citizens. Those billions of tax dollars are needed to build up
and to support a standing "world army."

U.S. Armed Forces Prepare For Urban Conflict

Regrettably, what is left of America's armed forces will also
be ordered by the White House into action to put down the
rebellion and patrol the streets. For over five years now, the
military has been preparing for this grim moment. In Chicago,
Detroit and a score of other cities and towns across America,
armed forces units have been rehearsing and practicing for

"urban warfare" against the citizenry. In Jacksonville, Florida, the *Jacksonville Times-Union,* in July, 1998, carried this headline: *"Marines Seized Downtown."* The newspaper described a U.S. Marine Corps war game conducted in Jacksonville. The Marine Corps called their exercise *Urban Warrior,* and a spokesperson said their goal was to "wrest control of parts of the city."

Major Frank Luster explained that, "The Marines are undertaking Urban Warrior with the expectation that future wars are increasingly likely to be waged on city streets."[16]

From another reliable source comes this insightful dispatch on miliary preparations for bloody days ahead in the streets following an imminent economic collapse and the fall of Wall Street:

> The U.S. government is expecting and preparing for a meltdown on Wall Street in the very near future.
>
> On June 16, 1998, the Navy and Marine Corps conducted their annual strategy meeting entitled, "Current Strategy Forum." This year's meeting was held at the U.S. Naval War College in Newport, Rhode Island. According to David Bay of Cutting Edge Ministries, an official who was in attendance at the meeting reported that he was shocked by a sentence uttered by the Under Secretary of the Navy, if only for its remarkable candor.
>
> The source reported, "After speaking for about 30 minutes from his prepared notes, the U.S. Under Secretary of the Navy, the Honorable Jerry MacArthur, then began to answer questions. After answering several questions, Mr. MacArthur made this statement, apparently off the cuff: "Senior Military Pentagon officials have been working closely with senior officials at Wall Street to perfect several scenarios that could quickly be put into action once Wall Street crashes."
>
> Notice the Under Secretary did not say "could crash" or

"may possibly crash." He emphatically stated that the Pentagon is fully expecting it to crash. The U.S. government is preparing. Are you?[17]

What must we do to protect ourselves and our families and prepare for the coming *Days of Hunger, Days of Chaos*? That is the focus of our next chapter which offers you "Keys to Survival and Prosperity." What we must *not* do is remain complacent. We simply do not have that luxury.

When chaos overflows on the streets of America, the Illuminati will be thrilled beyond measure. How many times have they and their antecedents attempted to establish a world system of control, only to be turned back in abject failure? Finally, they will have the pretext and possess the means to accomplish their vain ambitions. Finally, the whole world is at their feet, begging for bread and clamoring for security, safety, and life.

Looking back someday after the coming tough times have passed, we might conclude that, if only the Church establishment had not become lukewarm and apostate, if only it had not joined hands with the idol worshipers of America's globally-embraced culture, things would have been different. But minus the power of the Gospel, nothing could have been done to salvage our late, great nation, the United States of America.

It was the remarkable and venerable 19th century statesman, Daniel Webster, who once wrote what could one day become America's sad epitaph. Noting the advancing forces of corruption in the midst of an ever-diminishing and complacent Christian Church, Webster lamented:

> If the power of the gospel is not felt throughout the length and breadth of the land, anarchy and misrule, degradation and misery, corruption and darkness, will reign without mitigation or end.[18]

"But ye brethren, are not in darkness, that that day should overtake you as a thief.... For God hath not appointed us to wrath, but to obtain salvation by our Lord Jesus Christ." (I Thessalonians 5:4,9)

⅋ 12 ⅋

Your Keys to Survival and Prosperity

The herculean efforts of government bureaucrats to warehouse, control and distribute food supplies according to individual need will not succeed. Bureaucratic ineptitude and incompetence, combined with the sinister aims of government rulers, will result in a horrendously debilitating, worldwide famine. Riots, burnings, and murders will ensue as an angry and starving population grow ever more frustrated and alarmed. Desperation and hunger shall breed never before witnessed levels of violence.

The amazing thing about the coming great food shortages in America and around the globe is that they can be foreseen in advance. We know that worldwide food deprivation will occur because it is prophesied in the Holy Bible: "We have also a more sure word of prophesy; whereunto ye do well that ye take heed, as unto a light that shineth in a dark place." (*II Peter 1:19*)

The Sign of Thy Coming

It was Jesus Christ our Lord Himself who chronicled the events of the last days. His disciples came to Christ privately, as he sat upon the Mount of Olives, and asked of Him, "Tell us, when shall these things be? and what shall be the sign of thy coming, and of the end of the world?" (*Matthew 24:3*) In response, Jesus gave them—and us—an exact road map of future events to occur:

> And Jesus answered and said unto them, Take heed that no man deceive you. For many shall come in my name, saying, I am Christ; and shall deceive many. And ye shall hear of wars and rumours of wars: see that ye be not troubled: for all these things must come to pass, but the end is not yet. For nation will rise against nation, and kingdom against kingdom: and there shall be famines and pestilences...(*Matthew 24:4-7*)

We have certainly had false christs, and wars and rumours of wars. Nation after nation has risen up against neighbors. And there have been many famines and pestilences these past two millennia. But, our Lord said these things would escalate in the last days, and things would get so bad that if it were not for His return, no one would be spared. All the world's peoples would perish.

"But he that shall endure to the end, the same shall be saved," Christ said, "...and then shall the end come." (*Matthew 24:13, 14*)

The famine and pestilences to ravage the world just prior to the end shall be the most severe in history. The entire population will be gravely in peril. Look at what the prophet Joel said about the great catastrophe to hit our crops of food:

The field is wasted, the land mourneth; for the corn is wasted: the new wine is dried up, the oil languisheth. Be ye ashamed, O ye husbandmen; howl, O ye vinedressers, for the wheat and the barley; because the harvest of the field is perished. The vine is dried up, and the fig tree languisheth; the pomegranate tree, the palm tree also, and the apple tree, even all the trees of the field, are withered away from the sons of men. (*Joel 1:10-12*)

Alas for the day! For the day of the Lord is at hand, and as a destruction from the Almighty shall it come. Is not the meat cut off before our eyes, yea, joy and gladness from the house of our God? The seed is rotten under their clods, the garners are laid desolate, the barns are broken down; for the corn is withered. How do the beasts groan! The herds of cattle are perplexed, because they have no pasture; yea, the flocks of sheep are made desolate. (*Joel 1:15-18*)

Note that these things transpire as the time of Christ's return draws near. Famine and pestilence are judgements against the inhabitants of Earth who have rejected God's love. Sinners who have not repented and been saved by the grace of God will pay dearly for their disregard for truth and justice.

As A Snare Shall It Come

In *Luke 21:35* we see that when the world's food supplies dry up and men and women begin to suffer from starvation, it will come as a great surprise to them: "For as a snare shall it come on all them that dwell on the face of the earth."

We have been assured by the White House and by Wall Street that good times are permanent fixtures of society. Oh sure, we are told, occasionally there will be small blips in the flow of prosperity—temporary recessions and financial hurdles. But, the power brokers confidently assure us, these are just minor obstacles on the way to Utopia. And so, mankind races with blinders on down the yellow brick road toward

our destiny of an economic and planetary Waterloo.
Remember, however, Jesus' words: "...they be blind leaders
of the blind. And if the blind lead the blind, both shall fall
into the ditch." (*Matthew 15:14*)
The Apostle Paul warned that, "The day of the Lord so
cometh as a thief in the night. For when they shall say,
Peace and safety; then sudden destruction cometh upon
them...and they shall not escape." (*I Thessolonians 5:2-3*)
Christians, however, are cautioned to be sober, to stay
awake, so that they be not taken by surprise:

> But ye, brethren, are not in darkness, that that day should
> overtake you as a thief...For God hath not appointed us to
> wrath, but to obtain salvation by our Lord Jesus Christ. (*1
> Thessalonians 5:4, 9*)

Christians are Survivalists

It is the will of God that His people prepare in advance for
the momentous crisis to come. Believers are not complacent,
but are aware of the dangerous times in which they live.
God's people are survivors. Noah was a *survivalist*. So was
Lot, and so was Joseph, and so was Elijah. Because of their
foresight and due to the advance warning given them by
God—they survived and prospered.
Wise Christians are, therefore, *survivalists* who operate
from a perspective of *no fear* of the terror to come. But
Christians are not like the unsaved and unwise, would-be
"survivalists" who cringe in fright because of the horrors
they imagine may come upon them. These shivering creatures
stock up on firearms and dry food and head for their mountain
cabin, cave or foxhole in the wilderness. They reject the
Bible and godly counsel and, instead, are motivated by gossip
and hearsay. Their ears tingle when they are fed disinformation
about pseudo-crises. Such men are constantly running from
they know not what, to they know not where!
But the Christian man and woman is serene in knowledge.

They prepare for *real* emergencies and do not listen to chicken-little and his like. *Ezekiel 38:7* says: "Be thou prepared, and prepare for thyself, thou, and all thy company that are assembled unto thee, and be thou a guard unto them."

Such men and women have faith in God's provision and in His divine protection. But they also know of the faith teachings of *James 2:17,* "Faith, if it hath not works, is dead." By works, said James, is faith made manifest.

Dealing with Scorners

Now, any time someone from a biblical perspective speaks of hunger and famine to grip America, such a person will be mocked and scorned. We're all aware of the horrible droughts, famines and deaths from starvation that have occurred in places like Somalia, Chad, Burundi and Ethiopia in Africa. But most Americans simply would protest and say, "Oh no, not here, not in stable America."

I understand that kind of attitude. I've gone with my wife Wanda to the supermarket and it's unbelievable. The aisles of food are bulging with brand after brand and type after type of everything from chocolates, cookies, and fruit, to vegetables, meats and canned products. There are shelf upon shelf and freezer after freezer of bottles and jars and packages of frozen food. It boggles the mind.

And so, anyone who would say that all of these things will definitely one day soon dry up and the shelves will become empty will be looked upon with disdain, if not with a wry smile. A man sounds like a raving, crazy maniac to even suggest such a foolish thing. But my friends, take heed. Because we have God's prophetic Word, we *know* that there *will* be days of hunger and days of chaos.

As we discussed earlier in this book, in *Revelation 6:5* we find an eye-opening prophecy pointing to the problem of food:

And when he had opened the third seal, I heard the third beast say, Come and see. And I beheld, and lo a black horse; and he that sat on him had a pair of balances in his hand. And I heard a voice in the midst of the four beasts say, A measure of wheat for a penny, and three measures of barley for a penny; and see thou hurt not the oil and the wine.

Here we have a worrisome image of a black horse, a sign of great evil, and the one who sits on this black horse has a pair of balances. He's measuring something, and what is it he's measuring? Wheat and barley, and then there's the oil and the wine—these things are being held in the balance. Evidently, these natural resources of food, oil and wine are going to be very precious commodities in the last days. People will be very concerned about the prices and availability of those commodities in the last days. Food is going to move to the center stage of world anxiety very soon.

The black horse is followed by the pale horse, who ushers in Death and Hell and hunger:

And I looked, and behold a pale horse: and his name that sat on him was Death, and Hell followed with him. And power was given unto them over the fourth part of the earth, to kill with sword and with hunger and with death. (*Revelation 6:8*)

There's no doubt about it; we prophetically see a great food crisis developing, and Death and Hell follow that pale, sickly horse. A great, hell-caused famine will bring death to people on the Earth, to exactly one-fourth of all the inhabitants. That will be one and one-half billion people if we consider the present population of Earth. Now, the population of the United States is approximately 250 million. That means, my friends, that six times the population of the United States of America will die worldwide and that in the U.S.A. alone, over 60 million will die of hunger and malnutrition.

Food As a Means of Control

Food will also be used as a means of control. What better

thing? We can do without stereos, televisions and boats, without furs and jewels. We can do without our magazines and fancy cars, and discard our computers. We can scale down on our houses and our apartment homes. But food is something you have to have, it is essential. How better to control people than through the sale and exchange of food and groceries?

And so, we read in *Revelation 13* that every man, every woman, every child will be required to take the mark. Either in their forehead or in their right hand, and no man may buy nor sell save he that has the mark, or the name or number of the beast. In other words, if you will sell your soul to Satan and take the mark, you'll be able to buy food.

So we must believe the accuracy of the Bible in prophesying of food shortages, and warning about the controlling of the people through the selling and buying of food supplies. Still, this sounds very odd because today, in America, an oasis of strength, we seemingly have so much food. And many of us are gaining weight around the midriff. It is unbelievable, inconceivable even, that there will be days of hunger, days of chaos. But, I'm telling you: things *will* change, and the astounding process has *already* begun.

When Will Jesus Return?

We do know that the New World Order elite has planned that the new millennium will usher in their time of great power and authority. But God may have other plans. He alone is in charge of the itinerary and timing of events. You see, Satan knows his time is short, it says so in the book of *Revelation*, and he's furious. Thus, he goes about doing great damage in the last days. He knows that the prophetic time clock is ticking away; yet, Satan does not know exactly when Jesus will return again. Neither do I, neither do you, nor do the angels in heaven. Jesus said only the Father knows when Christ will return.

But Christ said we *can* discern the *season* for His coming again. When we consider the world around us, we realize that His coming must be at hand—all the signs are there. It behooves us, therefore, to prepare. Remember, Noah knew not the day when the flood would come, but he obeyed God. In preparation he built a gigantic ark on dry land. When the rains came, Noah and his family were lifted up in the ark. Untold numbers refused to believe. They did not prepare, and they perished.

In Egypt, the Pharaoh believed Joseph's godly interpretation of his dream—and he and his people prepared years in advance for the coming famine. Egypt prospered during bad times while many perished. Let us, also, be wise and, believing in God, prepare for coming hard times.

How blessed we are as Christians to receive the warning in advance and have sufficient time to prepare. I would like to propose that we prepare ourselves and our families on two fronts: spiritual and physical. By far, the spiritual dimension is the most vital and important.

Spiritual Preparation

Spiritual preparation for famine is really the preparation of food for the soul. First in our preparation is the recognition that we have nothing to fear or be worried about, because God has already arranged each day of our lives. All our steps are foreseen and planned by Him (*Proverbs 16:9*).

In the Lord's Prayer is wisdom: "Thy will be done..." If God is for us, and we are walking in His path, following His will, who can succeed against us?

In the Lord's Prayer, we pray: "...*give us this day our daily bread.*" *Daily* bread! Doesn't the Lord answer our prayers? Yes, of course! And Jesus Himself instructed us to beseech the Lord each day for our food for that day. He can and will provide for us.

It is certain that Bible-believing Christians will be denied food by Big Brother's despicable, God-hating bureaucrats. They cannot punish God, so they figure they'll use us as proxies. But they will not ultimately succeed. From studying

Isaiah 33:16, we know that for the man and woman of God: "He shall dwell on high: his place of defense shall be the munitions of rocks: bread shall be given him." We can trust and rely on the Lord to shield, protect, and feed us in hard times:

> Behold, the eye of the Lord is upon them that fear him, upon them that hope in his mercy; to deliver their soul from death, and to keep them alive in famine. Our soul waiteth for the Lord: He is our help and our shield. For our heart shall rejoice in him, because we have trusted in his holy name. Let Thy mercy, O Lord, be upon us, according as we have hope in thee. (*Psalms 33:18,22*)

How profound also is *Psalms 52:1*: "The goodness of God endureth continually." In this verse we find assurance that the Lord will never leave us, that his goodness and love endures forever. We should never think that we have been abandoned. God will never do that. Draw close to Him and you will discover He is beside you "continually."

Faith is essential to the Christian in hard times. Because God is always with us, we should be strong and stand in the faith. Undoubtedly, during the coming era, as faith is virtually extinguished on this planet, it will be difficult to remain strong in the face of adversity. You and I will be mocked for our faith, and we will be tempted to compromise. However, God will give us the strength we need, at the exact time we need it, to stand.

With faith, we can foresee the future. This is a dynamic way to prepare. We should always include in our prayers a plea to the Lord to help us to know in advance what is in store for our lives. God often gives His children a picture of what is to occur. We ought not be taken unaware of world events that could severely impact our lives. With study on our parts and insight from God, we won't. We read in *Proverbs 22:3*: "A prudent man foreseeth the evil, and hideth himself: but the simple pass on, and are punished."

It is true that God does not promise the Christian that he

or she will not experience tribulation and sorrow. We may not be spared bad times and suffering. But God knows our limits and our endurance. He will not allow more than we can bear. Nor will God Himself be the instrument of any pain or anguish. The world hates the true Christian. We are a shining light, and the disciple of Satan craves the darkness and despises the brightness and shining of the Christian who walks with God.

Still, even if we are persecuted and tormented, we know that He is with us to comfort us. We also know that all things work together for good for them that love the Lord. And what we experience on this Earth will be only a tiny drop in the sea of eternity:

> Let not your heart be troubled: ye believe in God, believe also in me. In my Father's house are many mansions: if it were not so, I would have told you. I go to prepare a place for you. And if I go and prepare a place for you, I will come again, and receive you into myself; that where I am, there ye may be also. (*John 14:1-3*)

Physical Preparation

While the nourishment of the spiritual person is paramount and takes precedence, there is absolutely nothing wrong with making *physical* preparations for hard times. Again, the accounts of great Old Testament examples like Noah and Joseph come to mind. Noah believed and had faith in God, and he proved it by physical action—the building of an ark and the collection of animals for the coming journey. Joseph for his part knew God would see him through the tough times, even when he was unjustly cast into prison. And when God gave advance word of the approaching famine, Joseph prepared by storing up food in the Pharaoh's storehouses. He proved in action that he believed God's advance warnings.

Now, you and I have the opportunity to prove with our action that we believe the advance warning God is giving us.

I suggest you pray and ask God exactly what He would have you to do to prepare—then, DO IT!

It would take an entire separate book to detail the many things that you and I can do to physically prepare for the coming great food shortages. My ministry offers a number of tapes, videos, and other materials to assist you in this regard. (For information or for a free subscription to our monthly newsletter, phone the ministry toll free, (800) 234-9673, or write to: Texe Marrs, 1708 Patterson Road, Austin, Texas 78733.) I would like to offer here just a few suggestions for your consideration:

Ten Steps for Physical Preparation

1. *Get Out of Financial Debt.* Yes, I know this is easier said than done. With mortgages, credit cards, and all the other debt the average consumer is saddled with, many just cannot see their way to getting rid of debt. Nevertheless, I recommend you mount a superhuman effort, praying to the Father for the strength and means to escape the debt cycle. The Holy Bible, in its great wisdom, reminds us: "The rich ruleth over the poor, and the borrower is servant to the lender." (*Proverbs 22:7*)

2. *Store Up Food.* A number of ministries and companies now offer dry food systems at an excellent value. For example, my own ministry offers dehydrated food in sealed cans and packages that is truly delicious and has a durable shelf life of several years. Then again, there are dry and canned foods available at your local supermarket that you can acquire and store away. With computers and modern inventory systems, the average supermarket operates on the accounting principle, "just in time." This means that barely enough supplies of food are stocked, and the grocery store orders replacements just in time to meet continuing demand. But when an emergency comes and trucks don't deliver, that means big trouble for

customers who do not have in their food pantries a sufficient reserve. I really believe it essential for a family to have a minimum of 60 to 90 days food on hand at all times.

A family garden is also a wonderful idea, and canning your own food for later use can provide superb benefits.

Remember, also, that Christians and patriots will be denied food and essentials during hard times once the universal "mark of the beast" system is inplemented. Anyone who takes the mark in order to obtain food will be damned forever. So take heed and prepare.

3. *Store Up Water.* If you have your own water well, fantastic! Of course, if your well needs power, and the power company is out of business permanently or temporarily, you're out of business. In that case, you should consider acquiring a generator that operates on diesel, gasoline, or other fuel. A standby generator is a wonderful thing to have around if the electric power for your home goes out, too.

If you have no water well, then begin filling up clean and sterilized containers with water. Distilled water is best, but tap water is OK, too. Use a teaspoon of hydrogen peroxide or a half teaspoon of bleach per gallon to keep the water pure and free of bacteria.

4. *Store Up Essentials.* When the crunch comes, make sure you have essentials—batteries, fuel oil, candles, paper towels or cloths, tools, wrapping tape, soap, basic medicines and prescription medicines, first aid supplies, etc. How often do we hear of a hurricane heading for a coastal city in Florida, Texas,or North Carolina and grocery and hardware store shelves being cleaned out and emptied in hours? Don't find yourself in this predicament—prepare now.

5. *Stay Healthy.* Preventative medicine is always the best. If you need a tooth filled or pulled—do it now. When hard times come, a dentist may not be available—or his office won't have the electric power for him to operate his high tech drills and instruments, etc. Likewise, if

you've been putting off that minor operation to remove that ingrown toenail, do it as soon as possible. That goes for any minor—or major—surgical procedure.

It goes without saying that in preparation for hard times our bodies should be fit and in condition. That doesn't necessarily mean jogging 10 miles a day, but it might be a terrific idea to *walk* a mile or two a day.

We should eat right. Sugars, sweets and starches— well, you and I know they're not good for us. In fact, they're deadly. And alcohol—I think it's only useful to pickle things, don't you?

6. *Secure Hard Copies of Important Documents.* During crises, you may find it difficult, or nigh impossible, to obtain copies of your marriage or birth certificates, mortgage and loan agreements, IRS and service records, deeds and titles—keep a copy in a safe, secure place.

7. *Evaluate Where You Live.* Living in the country is going to be best, especially to avoid riots and plundering by mobs, expected to occur in cities and adjoining suburbs. But not everyone has the financial ability or the opportunity to live in the country As a minimum, ask yourself how you will protect yourself and your lived ones in time of trouble. What will you do—right where you live now— if the water and power system goes out?...If local food stores lock their doors?...If 911 stops answering and you can't phone the police or an ambulance?

8. *Obtain Firearms and Ammunition for Protection.* Notice, I said: "for protection." If law and order breaks down, you will have to personally bear the responsibility of protecting your family from some very bad people who mean you harm. Don't be a foolish Polyanna. A godly and wise man takes care of his family—an infidel does not because he is either careless, lazy, fearful, unprepared, stupid, or *all* of these things. When God put in His Ten Commandments, "Thou shalt not kill," he meant, "Don't murder an innocent

person in cold blood—don't be a Cain!" God never intended for Christians to volunteer their families to be tortured, raped, and killed by violent criminals!

9. *Train Yourself on Basics.* Self-reliance is going to prove a valuable asset when the bad times come. Can you sew, farm, hunt, or fish? Do you know how to construct a temporary privy? Can you repair essential things around the house—plumbing fixtures, electrical outlets, etc.? Most people are totally dependent on others for all their needs. You should prepare to help yourself and your family in times of trouble. Besides, learning new skills and the basics of self-reliance can be entertaining, useful, and fun!

10. *Grow as a Family.* When seemingly almost everyone but God forsakes you, it's great to have the love of your immediate family. Don't let the cares of this world get in the way of developing the nurture of family life. Take time now to let your wife, husband, and children know how much you love them. Let them know you'll always be there for them, no matter what the world throws your way. Pray together and grow together as a family under the guidance of the Holy Spirit.

* * * * * * * *

The above is just a primer. I pray you will obtain my monthly newsletter and other resources offered by the ministry and investigate further into what you can do to insure your survival and prosperity in the coming hard times.

You Can Lead a Prosperous Life Even in Hard Times

Did I say, *"prosperity?"* Yes, I certainly did. It is my firm conviction that Christians should strive not only to survive but to prosper in hard times. Prosperity *may* mean physical success and riches, and God does prosper some Christians—

though only a few—bringing them material riches and wealth. But, the person who would be rich brings upon himself misery and trouble. Remember, the Apostle Paul said he was content no matter what his circumstances. Even in prison, he was satisfied, for the Lord was with him.

Are the super-rich who reject the Lord and who persecute God's people "prosperous?" Maybe, by the world's standards. But, not by God's! These men and women are in dire poverty and they don't even know it:

> Because thou sayest, I am rich, and increased with goods, and have need of nothing; and knowest not that thou art wretched, and miserable, and poor, and blind, and naked. (*Revelation 3:17*)

It may be that God will soon strip from us almost everything we own. Yet, we should always praise Him and thank Him for his goodness. To the world, this may seem hollow and foolish, but to the wise, it is wisdom, and it is life. Whatever our circumstances, He will see us through. He is our living bread.

Moreover, God has preordained all things for our good. So that, all in all, we shall live gloriously and victoriously forever and ever. Do you seek true prosperity? You'll find it in God's word and on your knees in communication with Him. In Him are incalculable riches that cannot be possessed by the Illuminati or the so-called supermen or celebrities of this world; nor can such base men and women even know of such riches.

A Helping Hand to Others

One way to help insure your own prosperity is to care for others. In the coming hard times, Christians should not withdraw from the world and become hermits. We are *in* the world, but not *of* the World. This means, in part, that we must do our utmost to warn others—especially the unsaved—

of the disaster that lies ahead. This planet is like the ship, *Titanic,* and a deadly iceberg of hunger, pestilence, and death lies straight ahead. In such a time, what better gift can we offer our neighbors and loved ones than the gift of salvation?

I encourage Christians to also share, inasmuch as is possible, food and essentials with those in desperate need. Inquire into the example of Joseph in Egypt who, in charity, gave of his bounty to his brethren, even though they had once deserted him and left him for dead. Though our own families come first, if we have the means to assist, we cannot neglect those less fortunate. We read in *Proverbs 22:9,* "He that hath a bountiful eye shall be blessed; for he giveth of his bread to the poor."

A Time to Every Purpose

In *Ecclesiastes 3:1-2,* Solomon wrote these magnificent and profound words: "To everything there is a season, a time to every purpose under the heaven: a time to be born, and a time to die; a time to plant, and a time to pluck up that which is planted."

In God's perfect timing, we shall be visited by *Days of Hunger, Days of Chaos.* I believe the signs clearly demonstrate that we are on the very threshold of a tragic season of bitter harvests. Yet, God has His purpose in these things. Blessed with God's love and mercy, trusting in His majesty, we will endure—and prosper! An eternity of hope and wonder and joy awaits us, just beyond the horizon. This gray season shall soon pass into an ill-remembered and forgotten yesterday and we shall joyously be with the Lord for all our days:

Eye hath not seen, nor ear heard, neither entered into the heart of man, the things which God hath prepared for them that love Him. (*I Corinthians 2:9*)

"...lo, I am with you always, even unto the end of the world." (*Matthew 28:20*)

FOOTNOTES AND REFERENCES

Introduction: "Behold A Pale Horse"

1. Louis McFadden, quoted in *The Federal Reserve Hoax*, by Wickcliffe B. Vennard (Boston: Forum Publication Co., 1934), p. 39.

Chapter 1: The Coming Great Hunger

1. A.K. Chesterton, *The New Unhappy Lords: An Exposure of Power Politics* (Great Britain).

2. Jean-Marie LePen, quoted in *Spotlight* newspaper, June 24, 1996, pp. 10-11, "French Populist Visits Iraq, Raps American-Led Embargo."

3. *Ibid.*

4. Taylor Caldwell, quoted in *The Review of the News*, May 29, 1974; reprinted in *The New American*, May 1, 1995.

5. *Ibid.*

6. *Ibid.*

7. *Ibid.*

8. *The New International Economic Order,* booklet published by World Goodwill, New York, New York, September 1980.

9. Ervin Lazlo, quoted in Dennis L. Cuddy, *Now is The Dawning of the New Age New World Order* (Oklahoma City, Oklahoma: Hearthstone Publishing Ltd., 1991), p. 265.

10. *Straight Talk* newsletter (Pigeon Forge, Tennessee), October 21, 1998.

Chapter 2:   Famine and Pestilence Are Predetermined

1. For example, see Texe Marrs' books, *Dark Majesty: The Secret Brotherhood and the Magic of A Thousand Points of Light* (Austin, Texas: Living Truth Publishers, 1992) and *Circle of Intrigue: The Hidden Inner Circle of the Global Illuminati Conspiracy* (Austin, Texas: Living Truth Publishers, 1995).

2. Catherine Bertini, Executive Director, United Nations World Food Program, quoted in *Cherinth Chronicle*, July-September 1998, p. 22. Also see Michael Coffman, *Saviors of The Earth?* (Chicago: Northfield Publishing, 1994).

3. See Texe Marrs, *Dark Secrets of the New Age* (Crossway Books, 14th printing, 1995), pp. 11- 23.

4. Mary Bailey, 1970, quoted by Dennis L. Cuddy, *Now Is the Dawning of the New Age New World Order* (Oklahoma City: Hearthstone Publishing, p. 166).

5. Malachi Martin, from a list of questions and answers that Simon & Schuster (New York), publisher of Martin's book *Keys of This Blood* (1990), sent out as part of a press kit.

6. Carroll J. Quigley, *Tragedy and Hope: A History of the World in Our Time* (New York: Macmillan, 1966).

7. Texe Marrs, *Project L.U.C.I.D.: The Beast 666 Human Control System* (Austin, Texas: Living Truth Publishers, 1996).

8. Carroll J. Quigley, *op. cit.*

9. Randall Baer, *Inside the New Age Nighmare* (Huntington House Publishers, 1989).

10. H.G. Wells, *The Shape of Things to Come*

Chapter 4: Big Brother is Watching Our Food Supplies

1. Barry Smith, "Farmers Under Attack," *Omega Times* (New Zealand), p. 11.

2. *Ibid.*

3. *Ibid.*

4. The *London Daily Telegraph*, quoted in *Ibid.*

5. *Ibid.*

6. Lawrence Patterson, *Criminal Politics*, October 1994, p. 36.

7. See Articles 8a and 8e of the Biological Diversity Treaty. Also see Bureau of Land Management Internal Working Document on Ecosystem Management, April 30, 1994; Michael S. Coffman, *Saviors of the Earth?* (Chicago: Northfield Publishing, 1994); and David A. Russell, *Who Is Leading the Attack on American Liberty?* (Crestview, Florida: Citizens for Consitutional Property Rights, 1997).

8. "Patent Issues Affect Everyone," *Seed Midan* newsletter, published by the Abundant Seed Foundation, Port Townsend, Washington, Fall 1995.

9. "Seeds of Conflict," *Time* magazine, September 25, 1995.

10. Ken Corbitt, "Seeds: Survival or Servitude?," *Nexus* magazine, August/September 1994, p. 14.

11. *Ibid.*

12. *Ibid.*

13. Victor Smart, "Spies in Sky Zero in on Farm Cheats," *The European* July 30, 1993, p. 1.

14. Albert Gore, Jr., speech reported in *Associated Press*, May 26, 1995.

15. *Ibid.*

16. "The Hills Have Eyes," *The Nature Conservancy* magazine, March/April 1998, p. 19.

17. *Ibid.*

18. "Satellite Mapping Reaps Higher Crop Yields," *Machine Design*, March 21, 1996, pp. 54-58.

Chapter 5:   Demon Seeds—The Seed Conspiracy
and the Terminator Gene

1. Jim Hightower, "USDA's Barren Seed," published on the internet; reprinted in *The Echo*, April 24-30, 1998 and in *Orlando Weekly*, April 23, 1998.

2. Cath Blackledge, "The Green Revolution," *The European* newspaper, May 19-24, 1998, pp. 20-21. Also see "Agr Evo Buys Seeds of Success," *The European*, October 5-11, 1998, p. 25.

3. Scott Kilman and Susan Warren, "Old Rivals Fight for New Turf—Biotech Crops," *The Wall Street Journal*, May 27, 1998.

4. Ken Corbitt, "Seeds: Survival or Servitude?," *Nexus* magazine, August and September 1994.

5. Geri Guidetti, "Seed Terminator and Mega-Merger Threaten Food and Freedom," *The Jubilee* newspaper, July/August 1998, (Reprinted—orginally published on The Ark Institute's web site @ *http: www.arkinstitute.com*).

6. *Ibid.*

7. Jeff Baker, "Baker's Babylonian Briefs," *The Remnant Watch* newsletter, April 1998, p. 5.

8. Edward Hammond, "Terminator Technology Will Prevent Second-Generation Seed From Growing," *Media Bypass* magazine, May 1998, pp. 36-37. Also see Curt Anderson, *Weekly Farm* (*Associated Press*), "Patent for Sterile Seeds Sows Controversy," May 23, 1998.

9. Geri Guidetti, *op. cit.*

10. *Ibid.*

11. "Terminator Technology Will Prevent Second-Generation Seed From Growing," *Media Bypass* magazine, May 1998, pp. 36-37. Also see Curt Anderson, *Weekly Farm* (*Associated Press*), "Patent for Sterile Seeds Sows Controversy," May 23, 1998.

12. *Ibid.*

13. Jim Hightower, *op. cit.*

14. *Ibid.*

15. *Ibid.*

16. "In Defense of the Demon Seed," *The Economist* magazine, June 13-19, 1998.

17. Pastor Earl Jones, *Intelligence Newsletter*, September/ October 1998, p. 6.

18. *Ibid.*

Chapter 6: Global Cartel Controls and Manipulates World Food Supplies

1. Rudy Stanko, *The Score* (Gering, Nebraska: Institute for Christian Bankers, 1986).

2. "On the Lone Prairie, A Rancher Sees Peril in an Air Force Plan," *The Wall Street Journal*, September 15, 1998; pp. A-14.

3. Marcia M. Baker, "Cartel Control Created Problems Moving Grain," *The New Federalist*, October 16, 1996, p. 11.

4. *Ibid.*

5. *Ibid.*

6. *Ibid.*

7. T.R. Reid, *Feeding the Planet,* quoted in *National Geographic*, No. 4, October 1998.

8. Don McAlvany, *The McAlvany Intelligence Adviser* newsletter, September 1995, p. 12.

9. *Exegis* newsletter, June 1996, p. 3.

10. Robyn Meredith, "Archer Daniels Investors Launch Revolt," *USA Today*, October 20, 1995, p. B-1.

11. James Henry, *Indiana Agrinews*, Vol. 17, No. 20, February 2, 1996.

12. "Wheat Shortages Looming," *Toronto Globe and Mail*, July 14, 1995.

13. "Low Wheat Harvest Expected—50 Year Low," *Austin American-Statesman*, April 12, 1996, p. C-1.

14. "Loaf of Bread to Cost More," *The Toronto Star*, April 23, 1996, p. A-4.

15. "Agriculture Crisis Grows in Cattle and Cotton Areas," *The New Federalist*, January 22, 1996, p. 8.

16. "Drought Could Mean Disaster for Grain Elevators, "*Austin American-Statesman*, June 1, 1996, p. D-1.

17. Tracy Reeves, "World Food Shortages Grows as Surplus Stocks Dwindle," *Knight-Ridder World Bureau*, December 17, 1995.

18. Jonathan Fuerbringer, "Production Pressure Rises as Commodity Prices Fall," *The New York Times*, August 28, 1998, p. D-8.

19. *Associated Press, Austin American-Statesman,* September 13, 1998, p. A-2.

20. "India Onion Crisis Peels Away Trust," *Associated Press*, reported in *Austin American- Statesman*, October 11, 1998, p. A-10.

21. "Another Grim Year for North Korea," *Associated Press*, reported in *Austin American-Statesman*, October 11, 1998, p. A-10.

22. *Cherith Chronicles*, July-September 1998, p. 29.

Chapter 7:   The New Colonialism—Small Farmers Are Crushed

1. Texe Marrs, *Millennium: Peace, Promises, and the Day They Take Our Money Away* (Austin, Texas: Living Truth Publishers, 1990).

2. Laura Meckler, "Small Family Operations Decline" *(Associated Press)* in *Austin American- Statesman*, August 1996, p. D-1.

3. *Ibid.*

4. *Ibid.*

5. *Ibid.*

6. *Ibid.*

7. *Ibid.*

8. Charles Walters, *Acres USA*, quoted in *Spotlight* newspaper, October 12, 1998, p. 19.

9. *Spotlight*, October 12, 1998, p. 8.

10. *Ibid.*

11. *Ibid.*

12. Congressional Quarterly, quote in *Ibid.*

13. Blake Hurst, "Field of Dreams—Organic Agriculture Doesn't Pay the Seed Bills," *Policy Review*, Winter 1991, published by the Heritage Foundation.

14. *Ibid.*

15. Nelson Antosh "Soured On Dairy Work," *Houston Chronicle*, May 26, 1996, p. 2-E.

Chapter 8: "Food is Power!"—They Shall Control Food, Life, and Death

1. Catherine Bertini, quoted in *The McAlvany Intelligence Advisor*, February 1996, p. 9.

2. Uri Dowbenko, *The Nationalist Times*, October 1998.

3. George Orwell, *1984* (New York: Harcourt Brace Jovanovich, Inc., 1949).

4. Mikhail Gorbachev, *Perestroika: New Way of Thinking For Our Country and Our World.* Also see the discussion of *Perestroika* and Gorbachev in Texe Marrs' book, *Mystery Mark of the New Age* (Westchester, Illinois: Crossway Books, 1988).

5. Anatoly Golitsyn, *The Perestroika Deception: The World's Slide Toward the Second October Revolution* (New York: Edward Harle, 1995), p. 34.

6. See Texe Marrs' book *Big Sister is Watching You* (Austin, Texas: Living Truth Publishers, 1993).

7. Anatoly Golitsyn, *op. cit.*

8. Bob Trefz, *Cherith Chronicles*, July-September, p. 7.

9. Alice Bailey, *The Unfinished Autobiography* (New York/London: Lucis Publications, 1951).

10. *Ibid*, p. 231.

11. *The New International Economic Order*, World Goodwill Commentary, Number 14, September 1980.

12. Mihajlo Mesarovic and Edvard Pestel, *Mankind at the Turning Point* (New York: E.P. Dutton, 1974).

13. *Ibid.*

14. *Calvary Contender* newsletter, January 1, 1995, p. 1.

15. Tony Townsend, editor, *The Emergence,* October 1998.

16. Larry Bates, *The New Economic Disorder* (Orlando, Florida: Creation House Books, 1994), p. 30.

17. *Ibid.*

18. *Ibid*, pp. 30-32.

19. *The New International Economic Order, op. cit.*

20. *World Goodwill Bulletin*, November 1991.

21. *Ibid.*

22. *Ibid.*

Chapter 9: The New Civilization

1. Alice Bailey, *The Unfinished Autobiography* (New York/ London: The Lucis Trust, 1951).

2. President Bill Clinton, quoted in *The Prophetic Times;* Ray Payton, editor, December 1997.

3. Alvin and Heidi Toffler, *Creating A New Civilization* (Atlanta, Georgia: Turner Publishing, Inc., 1995).

4. *Ibid*, p. 8.

5. *Ibid*, p. 19.

6. *Ibid*, pp. 20-21.

7. *Ibid*, p. 33.

8. *Ibid.*

9. *Ibid*, pp. 90-91.

10. Karl-Otto Liebmann, "Blueprint for Managed Foodcare," *The Wall Street Journal*, January 10, 1996.

11. Mikhail Heller and Aleksandr Nekrich, quoted by William Norman Grigg, *The New American*, November 9, 1998, pp. 29-30.

12. *Ibid.*

13. "Tugwell Predicts New Regulations for Land With Federal Control," *Phillip County News*, Malta, Montana, January 4, 1934.

14. Dan P. Van Gorder, *Ill Fares the Land: The Famine Planned for America* (Boston/Los Angeles: Western Islands, 1966).

15. *Ibid*, p. 199.

16. *Ibid.*

17. Dr. John Coleman, *Grain and Food Cartels Wage War on America and Europe*; a report published by W.I.R., 25533 North Carson Street, Suite J-118, Carson City, Nevada 89706.

18. *The Scottish Rite Journal*, February 1993, pp. 31-33.

19. *Ibid.*

20. *Ibid.*

21. *Ibid.*

Chapter 10: Darkness Descending—Panic, Solutions, and the Restructuring of America

1. Bob Trefz, *Cherith Chronicle*, July-September 1998, p. 3.

2. *Ibid.*

3. David M. Bresnahan, World Net Daily, November 14, 1998.

4. Vera Stanley Alder, *When Humanity Comes of Age* (New York: Samuel Weiser, Inc., 1974), p. 13.

5. *Ibid*, p. 173.

6. Alice Bailey, *The Externalization of the Hierachy (New York, NY: Lucis Trust), p. 511.*

7. Very Stanley Alder, *op. cit.*

8. *Ibid*, pp. 45-49.

9. *Ibid*, p. 173.

10. Virgina Essene, *New Teachings for an Awakened Humanity* (Santa Clara, California: Spiritual Education Company, 1986), p. 165.

11. M. Scott Peck, *A Different Drum: Community-Making and Peace* (New York: Simon & Schuster, 1987), p. 17.

12. Vera Stanley Alder, *op. cit.*, p. 62.

13. *Ibid*, pp. 61-67.

14. *Ibid.*

15. John G. Gordon, *Veritas* newspaper, July, 1996.

16. See Texe Marrs, *Project L.U.C.I.D.—The Beast 666 Universal Human Control System* (Austin, Texas: Living Truth Publishers, 1996), pp. 131-140.

17. Suzan Jackson, quoted by Jackie Cox, "Is Mastering the Confusion of ISO 9000 the Key to the Marketplace?," *American Papermaker*, June 1992.

18. *The Daily Telegraph* (UK), August 7, 1995.

19. "Animal Magnetism," *The European*, April 13-19, 1998, p. 137.

Chapter 11: Food Riots, Chaos, Terror—The Collapse of Civilization

1. Donald McAlvany, *The McAlvany Intelligence Advisor* newsletter, October, 1998, p. 31.

2. Maurice Strong, UNCED Report, 1991; presented at the Earth Summit, 1992.

3. Larry Acker, quoted in, *The Reaper* newsletter, November 19, 1998, pp. 15-16.

4. *Ibid.*

5. Sidney Pollard, *Wealth and Poverty: An Economic History of the Twentieth Century* (Oxford, England/New York, NY: Oxford University Press, 1990), p. 214.

6. R.E. McMaster, *The Reaper*, November 19, 1998, p. 17.

7. Donald McAlvany, *The McAlvany Intelligence Adviser*, September 1995, p. 12.

8. *Ibid.*

9. See *Associated Press, Reuters News Service, Time,* and *Newsweek* magazines; circa 1998.

10. Reported in *Free American* news magazine, November 1997, p. 55.

11. *Pro-Farmer,* October 17, 1998. Also reported in *The Reaper* newsletter, November 5, 1998, p. 11.

12. *Time* magazine, September 7, 1998, pp. 32-34.

13. "North Korea: 3.5 Million Dead," *The Catholic World Report,* November 1998, p. 43.

14. Donald McAlvany, *The McAlvany Intelligence Adviser,* September 1995, p. 13.

15. Reported by Michael Reed, *The Community Standard,* Columbia, South Carolina, February 6, 1997.

16. "Marines Seize Downtown—Urban Warfare is Exercise's Aim," *Jacksonville Times—Union,* July 24, 1998.

17. Cliff Droke, *Last Days Journal,* September 1998, p. 6. Also: David Bay of Cutting Edge Ministries is on the World Wide web at address: *www.cuttingedge.org.*

18. Daniel Webster, quoted in *Today, The Bible and You,* January 1998, p. 5.

About the Author

Well-known author of the #1 national best-seller, *Dark Secrets of the New Age*, Texe Marrs has also written 36 other books for such major publishers as Simon & Schuster, John Wiley, Prentice Hall/Arco, Stein & Day, and Dow Jones-Irwin. His books have sold over two million copies.

Texe Marrs was assistant professor of aerospace studies, teaching American defense policy, strategic weapons systems, and related subjects at the University of Texas at Austin for five years. He has also taught international affairs, political science, and psychology for two other universities. A graduate *summa cum laude* from Park College, Kansas City, Missouri, he earned his Master's degree at North Carolina State University.

As a career USAF officer (now retired), he commanded communications-electronics and engineering units. He holds a number of military decorations, including the Vietnam Service Medal, and served in Germany, Italy, and throughout Asia.

President of RiverCrest Publishing, in Austin, Texas, Texe Marrs is a frequent guest on radio and TV talk shows throughout the U.S.A. and Canada. His monthly newsletter is distributed around the world, and he is also heard globally on his popular, international shortwave radio program, *Power of Prophecy.*

For Our Newsletter

Texe Marrs offers a *free* newsletter about Bible prophecy and world events, secret societies, the New Age movement, global conspiracies, the Illuminati, cults, and the occult challenge to Christianity. If you would like to receive a free subscription to this fascinating newsletter, please write to:

Power of Prophecy
1708 Patterson Road
Austin, Texas 78733

Please e-mail your newsletter request to: *prophecy@ texemarrs.com* or visit us at our internet web site: *http://www.texemarrs.com*

For Our Shortwave Radio Program

Texe Marrs' international radio program, **Power of Prophecy**, is broadcast weekly on shortwave radio and on selected AM/FM radio stations throughout the United States. The **Power of Prophecy** radio program is also available on the worldwide web (*internet real audio*). For more information or for a radio station log, please phone toll free (800) 234-9673 or write to: **Power of Prophecy**, 1708 Patterson Road, Austin Texas 78733.

For Our Internet Web Site

Texe Marrs' newsletter is published monthly on our web site. The web site has descriptions of all Texe Marrs' books and is packed with interesting, insight-filled articles and information about prophecy and world events. You also have the opportunity to order an exciting array of books, tapes, and videos through our on-line *Catalog and Sales Store*. Visit the web site today at *www.texemarrs.com.*